Compiled & Illustrated by
Melva Graham

First published 2003

Reprinted 2004, 2005 & 2007

This edition first published 2018

© Copyright by Melva Graham

171 Blackjack Road, Harcourt Vic 3453
Phone/Fax: 5474 2871

ISBN: 978-0-6481726-3-5

 A catalogue record for this book is available from the National Library of Australia

Acknowledgements

(This is where I do a bit of suckholin')

For this collection of Australian language I owe a lot to my dad who, although he had very little formal education, was a M.A.L. (Master of Aussie Lingo). Albert Ronald Clive, or Ar-Sey as the cheeky local postmistress used to call him, was a bit of a dag. However, he could charm the pants off a possum with his inventive turn of phrase.

I remember a time when he did a spot of **snake** charming as well!

Joe Blakes were a common sight around our joint each summer, but we usually only had to tell our fox terrier to "Go fox 'em!" and he'd beat the living daylights out of them. However, he'd gone walkabout the day that Dad cornered a snake under the haystack. Getting out his old squeezebox, he sat down near the haystack and played a few waltzes and foxtrots (he prided himself on being pretty good on the tootsies as well as the squeezebox).

Suddenly the snake shot out like greased lightning from under the haystack. Dad nearly died with his leg in the air! Dropping the squeezebox, he ran like billyo to get Mum. She came running with a folded lump of fencing wire that we kept by the back door, and soon polished off the snake.

"Blimey Charlie! I thought I was in more shit than a Werribee duck for a sec!" Dad exclaimed.

I also have to dip me lid to my hubby, known to his grandchildren as 'BB' (because of his habit of saying 'Be buggered!')

"Ta" also to those who filled up the blackboards at 'Woop-Woop' with remembered Aussie-isms. We got a kick out of them, and I hope you do, too.

Contents

	Intro	9
1.	Alcohol: Booze	11
2.	Anger: Goin' Berko	20
3.	Aussie, Aussie, Aussie	26
4.	Great Australian Adjectives	37
5.	Blokes and Sheilas	44
6.	Body Language	52
7.	Bouquets & Brickbats	65
8.	Clobber – Clothes	67
9.	Dead as …	71
10.	Dunnies	75
11.	Exclamations	81
12.	Faunal Lingo	85
13.	Food	88
14.	Galahs, Galoots & Idiots	97
15.	Mean & Miserly	103
16.	Nicknames	105
17.	Occupations	109
18.	Rabbit & Pork (Talk)	114
19.	Thingamabobs	118
20.	As Useful as …	120
21.	The Weather	122
22.	Money	127

Intro

Woop-Woop may not be listed in the postcode directory, but no longer is it merely a mythical place. We set it up to give us something to do to keep us out of mischief, and it's sort of grown like Topsy. (Did you know that **"to grow like Topsy"** means "to come out of nowhere and develop without encouragement?" It comes from the book "Uncle Tom's Cabin". Topsy was the little slave girl that said that she **"just growd. Don't think nobody ever made me".)**

If Andy hadn't found a use for his recycled treasures, he would have had to 'transfer' them back to the transfer station (modern euphemism for the 'dump'). When he offers to take me "out on the town", you can betcha life it'll be the town dump!

After the banksias we planted carked it overnight, we set about establishing a native garden, specializing in wattles. When visitors expressed disbelief in our claims of resident kangaroos on our block, we decided to 'create' some 'roos that would be more reliable in exposing themselves. A couple of emus, a wombat, and a dingo as well, and we were away.

Because we thought that we oughta be trying to keep our colourful and inventive language alive and kicking, we decided to fill our garden with sculptures and activities depicting Aussie sayings and humour (we even extended that idea to the seating throughout the garden.)

We built a boomerang-shaped gallery with 'gum trees' reaching up through the slanguage-covered tables, and 'plastered' the walls and ceiling with cartoons, colloquialisms and anything else to get you clued up on the lingo.

Someone once said that **"slang is the language that rolls up its sleeves and really gets to work on givin' you the drum."** It has also been called **"the poetry of the people"**, and Aussies are great exponents of poetry. After all, what other country has a special **POET'S DAY** each week?

Piss Off Early, Tomorrer's Saturday!

So's you can put your finger on a word and meaning quickly, this is a kind of **Finger-Saurus** (no band-aid needed)

So's I don't bore the pants off you, I've added a few poems, jokes and items of irrelevant rubbish as well.

Alcohol, and Being Boozed to the Eyeballs

Now Louis likes his native wine,
And Otto likes his beer;
The Pommy goes for half-and-half
Because it gives him cheer.
While Angus likes his whisky,
And Paddy likes his tot,
The Aussie has no national drink;
He likes the bloody lot!

Thought we'd start with a quick one.

How many men does it take to open a can of beer? None. It should be opened by the time she brings it.

Bit o' Bush Wisdom

When you're between waterholes,
If you dawdle you're dead –
Unless there's a pub in the middle.

It's no coincidence that two of our most popular songs are **"Pub with No Beer"** and **"I Love to Have a Beer with Duncan."** Aussies have a liking for **'bendin' the elbow'**, whether at the rubbidy, a barbie, or any get-together with mates.

Alcohol, and Being Boozed to the Eyeballs

Various forms of BOOZE (alcohol) ...

amber fluid	coldie
anotherie	drop
bombo	fire water
bubbly	gee and tee
champers / chateau de cardboard	giggle juice

grog (after an admiral nicknamed 'Old Grog' who diluted sailors' daily rations of rum with water)

heart starter	poison
hops	slops
hooch	snort
leg-opener	ten-ounce sandwich
jungle juice	turps
piss	vino
plonk	

The names for containers for alcohol served in the bar of the local watering hole vary from state to state. There are **bottles, butchers, cans, fives, handles, jugs, lady's waists, middies, mugs, pints, ponies, schooners, sevens, six-packs, slabs, stubbies, tinnies and tankards** – all designed to **'put a gut on ya.'** The ring pulls from beer cans are known as **'Territory confetti'**.

Did y' know that **'a shearer's cocktail'** is **'a dag in a glass of ewe piddle'**, or that if a beer's gone **'foxy'**, it's bad,

or that **'a barmaid's blush'** is rum mixed with raspberry cordial, or that **a Diamantina cocktail** is a mixture of Bundaberg rum, condensed milk and an emu's egg, or that **'Red Ned'** is cheap wine?

Well, whaddya know!

Drinking Establishments ...
(that's putting' on th' dog, eh?)

bloodhouse

boozer

local

pisser

rubbidy / rubbidy-dub

watering-hole

wet area (district where liquor is sold)

Many old Australian hotels had their own **'deadhouses'**, where paralytic customers were thrown into a shed so that they could sleep it off.

Drinking Law - The Shout ...

(No, we're not talking about the boys in blue. The **Law-According-to-Drinkers** is much more serious than that!)

The institution of treating friends to a round of drinks originated in pubs of the 1800's where you had to raise your voice in order to be heard. The one who shouted the collective order paid for it. It then became easier and more sociable to offer to '**shout**' or pay for the next round of drinks.

Anyone who leaves the circle before it's his turn to shout is:

lower than a snake's belly (and you can't get much lower than that!)

wouldn't shout in a shark attack (how miserable can you get?)

To tie up a dog / chain a pup / put it on the slate is to get drinks on credit.

The old warning to '**Mind your P's and Q's** is attributed to the practice of publicans chalking up on the slate the **P**ints and **Q**uarts consumed by drinkers.

Bit o' Bush Wisdom

If you drink alone,
It'll always be your shout.

Drinking Terms

bash the turps, bend the elbow, break-out, booze-up, down a few, drink like a fish, drink like it's going out of fashion, drink someone under the table, drink with the flies, have a drop of the doings, go on the scoot, grog on, guzzle, have a quickie, have one for the bitumen, have one for the road, have one too many, hit the booze / bottle / turps, Jimmy Woodser (lone drink or drinker), **on a bender, on the bottle / grog / piss / turps / ran-tan / slops, have a session, sink a few, stop one, tip the little finger, wet one's whistle**

Drunk As A Skunk

away with the birds / fairies / pixies

blind   **bombed**

blotto   **boozed**

brewer's droop (inability to raise an erection after drinking too much alcohol)

cut

drunk as a lord / monkey / owl

elephant's trunk (r.s.)   **flaked out**

full as a boot / bull's bum / fairy's phone book / family po / fart / fat woman's sock / goog / seaside dunny on Boxing Day / state school hat-rack / tick

had a few too many

had a skinful

half a sheet to the wind

half shot

high as a kite

history

hung-over
in the grip of the grape
legless
lit up like a Christmas tree
loaded
merry
molly the monk
off his face
on his ear
paralytic
pickled
pie-eyed
pinko
pissed as a cricket / fart / newt / parrot / picket
out of one's brain
plastered
primed
rolling drunk
rotten

shickered
shot
sizzled
sloshed
smashed
spaced out
stonkered
tanked
three-parts-gone
tiddly
tipsy
tired and emotional
unable to scratch himself
under the influence
under the weather
well-oiled
write-off
zonked

Bit o' Bush Wisdom

To the average Australian
there's only one evil worse than drink –
and that's thirst.

Heavy Drinkers ...

alkie / alco

booze artist / boozer

dipso

lush

piss-head

piss-pot

plonko

soak

sponge

two-pot screamer

winedot / wino (a 'dot' is a regular drinker of wine)

Toasts – More Power to Your Elbow!

Did y' know that the word **'toast'** came from the 16th century habit of putting a piece of toasted bread in the bottom of a tankard to collect the sediment and impurity at the bottom of the cup – musta been a crook brew in those days! When the brew improved they left out the toast, but the expression **'to drink a toast'** remained.

Cheers!

Down the hatch!

Here's lead in yer pencil!

Here's lookin' up yer kilt!

Here's mud in yer eye! (originally a racing term. The winner kicked mud into the eyes of those following)

Here's to 'ee! (popularized by Toohey's brews in New South Wales)

May y' live so long that there's no bugger left t' bury yer!

May all your troubles be little ones! (popular at weddings)

Did y' know that the custom of clinking glasses before drinking dates back thousands of years? It was thought that Old Nick might enter your body with the drink, and so by making a sound with your glass, you might be able to scare the daylights out of him! Some primitive tribes rang a bell *after* drinking – however, Old Nick might have already popped your cork by then!

Another explanation for clinking glasses was that the act of drinking alcohol invoked all the five senses – sight, smell, taste and touch – with the 'sound' completing the pleasure (bet you like the first explanation best!)

Under the Affluence of Inkahol ...

It's a cert that you'll **vomit** or –

bark at the lawn

call 'Ralph'

chunder

drive the porcelain bus

have a hair of the dog (hangover drink – burned hair of a mad dog was believed to be a cure for anything bad)

have a liquid laugh

make a long distance call on the big, white telephone

make a pavement pizza

mouth will feel like the bottom of a cocky's cage

park a tiger on the rug

give a technicolour yawn / yodel

spew

throw one's voice / throw up

Ruminating Riddles

How do you get an Aussie on the roof?
Tell him the drinks are on the house.

What's the difference between
an Australian wedding and an Australian funeral?
One less drunk!

Judge: "Officer, what made you think this man was drunk?"

Policeman: "Well, Your Honour, I didn't bother him when he staggered down the street and fell flat on his face, but when he put a twenty-cent piece in the mail-box, looked up at the town hall clock and said, "Good 'eavens, I've lost two pounds," I brought him in."

A well-endowed lass from Yagoona,
Worked in the local saloona,
But things didn't work out,
A 'born again' lout
Resented her boobs in his schooner.

Anger: Goin' Berko, Or Doin' Y' Chewie

Don't get off y' bike, I'll pick up y' pump! (calm down!)

Get out the wrong side of the bed? The left side is the wrong side of the bed according to early Roman superstition. It was believed that evil spirits lived on the left side, and their influence could be felt all day long – bit of a worry for partners sharing a double bed! Guess that's why the blokes always pick the right side of the fartsack.)

Aggro Or Bad-Tempered ...

aggers
crapped off
crooked on
crotchety
dark on
dirty on
fed up to the back teeth
fit to be tied
got one's knickers in a knot / twist
het-up
hot under the collar
huffy
jacked off
like a bear with a sore head
livid
maggoty
miffed
off one's face

off one's nut
off the planet
pissed off
prickly
riled up
ropeable
sarky
shirty
shitty
snaky
snitchy
snotty
sore
steamed up
stroppy
toey
up tight
worked up

Goin' to Town on Someone ...

Arse off, arsehole!

Bite your bum!

Damn and blast the muddy bucket of pitch!

Dip your left eye in hot cocky cack!

Drop dead!

Get stuffed!

Go bare your bum in Bourke Street!

Go teach your mother to suck eggs!

Go pull your chain!

Go take a running jump at yourself!

Hope all your chooks die and you can't sell your wire netting!

Hope your boobs turn into concrete and fall and smash your kneecaps!

Hope your earholes turn into arseholes and shit on your shoulder!

Hope your fingers turn to fish hooks and you get an itchy crutch!

I'll give you a knuckle sandwich!

I'll hang you on the wall for a picture!

I'll knock your teeth so far down your throat you'll have to stick a toothbrush up your arse to clean your teeth!

I'll rip off your arms, shove them in your ears, and ride you like a motor bike!

Anger: Goin' Berko, Or Doin' Y' Chewie

I'll rip your head off and shit down your neck!

I'll spiflicate you with the rough end of the pineapple!

I'll tear off your arm and belt you with the wet end!

I'll use your ears for door knockers!

I wouldn't piss on you if you were on fire!

Hope the fleas of a thousand camels infest your underwear!

Nickywoop! Piss off! Get lost!

POQ and DCB (Piss Off Quick and Don't Come Back!)

Pull your head in!

Put a sock in it!

Rack off hairy legs!

Scram, jam, or I'll spread you!

Stick it up your arse!

Stick it up your jumper!

Shut your cakehole!

Take a long walk off a short pier!

Up you! Up yours!

Up your bum, chum!

Up your date, mate!

Up your nose with a rubber hose – and twice as far with a chocolate bar!

Losin' One's Cool and Lettin' 'Em Have It ...

Anger: Goin' Berko, Or Doin' Y' Chewie

beat the living daylights out of 'em
beat the tripe out of 'em
blast hell out of 'em
blow a fuse
blow a gasket
blow one's stack
blow one's top
chuck a mental
chuck a spas
chuck a willie
chuck a wobbly
do one's block
do one's chewie
do one's cruet
do one's lolly
do one's nana
flip one's lid
flip out
fly off the handle
freak out
get off one's bike
get one's dander up
get one's tits in a tangle

Anger: Goin' Berko, Or Doin' Y' Chewie

give him a bit of the old one-two

give 'em Bondi

go bananas

go berko

go crook

go gonzo

go right off

go to market

have a barney / blue

have a stoush

rouse at 'em

sink the boot in

sink the slipper

spit the dummy

Ruminating Riddle

**How do you break an Aussie's finger?
Belt him in the nose.**

Bit o' Bush Wisdom

**The only way to end a blue
is to shout the other bloke a drink.**

A woman noted for her explosive temper and angry outbursts finally died. At the funeral, the coffin was lowered into the grave and the attendants started to shovel in the earth. Just as they were completing the job, a tremendous clap of thunder rent the air.

The woman's husband looked up and said, "Well, it looks like she's arrived."

Aussie, Aussie, Aussie, Oy! Oy! Oy!

(cry from Bazzaland, Down Under or Oz, not forgetting **'the arse end of the world'** – Paul Keating, PM)

If you can chant this then you're:

> **true blue**
> **ridgie-didge**
> **dinki-di**
> **dinkum Aussie**
> **fair dinkum**
> **as Australian as a meat pie**

The word **'dinkum'** comes from a north Lincolnshire dialect, meaning 'a share of work to be done'. Therefore, **'fair dinkum'** originally meant that the share of work should be fair. It has come to mean 'the genuine article' or 'true'.

'True blue' also comes from English, meaning 'totally loyal'. The colour 'blue' was a symbol of constancy dating back to medieval times. Aussies love to be referred to as **'true blue'**.

Australia was originally called *Terra Australis Incognita*, meaning 'unknown land of the south,'(if you remember a bit of Latin you'd know that *'Australis'* means 'south'). In the 17th century the Dutch came nosin' around, and called it 'New Holland'. When Captain Cook took a look in 1770, he claimed the eastern half for Britain, naming it New South Wales. The Brits later annexed the western half of the land because they

thought the French had their beady eyes on it. However, it was the explorer, Matthew Flinders who first used the word, **'Australia.'** Governor Macquarie thought this was a bonzer name, and we've been known as Aussies from Australia ever since.

Aussie Call ...

Coo-ee!

Originally a familiar call used by the aborigines, it was adopted by the colonists as well. Thus **'not within a coo-ee'** of something means 'not coming anywhere near it'.

Aussie Curse ...

"I hope your chooks turn into emus and kick your dunny door down!"

Aussie Farewell ...

Be seein' ya!   'Ooroo!   Ta-ta!   Seeya!   Seeya later! See you in the soup!   Well, I'm orf!   Wally-lu!

Often followed by – **Catch up with y' soon!**

Knock y' up sometime! Might bump into y' sometime!

Seeya sometime when you've nothing on!

Aussie Greeting ...

G'day! Owyergoinorright?

How's y' belly fer spots?

How's y' belly where th' pig bit yer?

How's y' bum fer grubs?

Talking of grubs:

Old Joe was leaning over the fence one day when the old lady next door was doing a spot of gardening. With the garden on her mind, she said, "You know, I often wonder which is worse – the aphis or the worms?"

"Can't 'elp yer, Missus," said Joe. "I ain't never 'ad aphis!"

Aussie National Anthem ...

Officially it's **'Advance Australia Fair.'** Well, that's the song that's trotted out for big events like cricket and footie matches, but most Aussies have a hard time remembering the words. However, when the band strikes up **'Waltzing Matilda,'** they can raise the roof off a tin shed!

Banjo Paterson's verse set to an old Scottish ballad caught the imagination of Aussies from the time that it was first performed in 1895. **'Mathilde'** in Germany was the equivalent of 'Sheila' in Ireland. **'Mathilde'** was also the word for 'blanket' or 'bedroll' which provided comfort when a female **'Mathilde'** wasn't available. The German word, 'waltzen' means 'aimless wandering', and so **'waltzing Matilda'** describes the lonely, aimless wandering of a swagman carrying his bedroll.

The songs, **'I Still Call Australia Home,'** and **'We are Australian'** are also pretty popular.

Aussie National Day: Australia Day ...

We have long been regarded as a bit unpatriotic compared to some other countries we know. However, just because we don't do a lot of flag-waving, doesn't mean we don't appreciate a long week-end holiday, with a few snags on the barbie. We even recognize our best scone makers and sportspersons by bestowing on them our own Orders of Australia!

January 26 (Australia Day), commemorates the landing of Captain Arthur Phillip and the convicts of the First Fleet at Sydney Cove in 1788. The day was known by different names in different states until in 1931 Victoria officially adopted the name, **'Australia Day'**, and the other states followed suit.

Anzac Day ...

On April 25 the men of the Australian and New Zealand Army Corps are remembered for their heroic deeds in World War 1. It has become a national day of remembrance for all servicemen and women in all wars. There is grim humour derived from these conflicts.

Anzac biscuits: hard biscuits sent to the troops – 'one of the most durable materials used in the war.'

Anzac button: a nail used to take the place of a trouser button.

Anzac soup: water polluted by a corpse

Anzac stew: hot water with a rind of bacon

Aussie National Flag ...

After the Commonwealth was inaugurated in 1901, a competition was held to find an Aussie flag. The winner incorporated the stars of the Southern Cross, which had been used previously by both the Australian Anti-Transportation League, and the diggers in the Eureka Stockade rebellion. Beneath the Southern Cross was a large, (now) seven-pointed star to represent the six states and the territories. In the left corner was the Union Jack – a bone of contention among republicans to the present day. You wouldn't read about it, but Aussies were actually discouraged from flying their own flag! Officially, until the Flags Act of 1953, when the Australian Blue Ensign was proclaimed the National Flag, the Commonwealth

Blue Ensign was regarded as an 'official' flag to be flown only by government bodies! Those shiny-bum bureaucrats have always been a bit slow on the uptake!

If you're **'flying the Aussie flag,'** your shirt tails are hanging out over your trousers.

Aussie National Flower ...

If you want to **'put on the dog,'** you can call our national floral emblem, the **'acacia'**, (from the Greek 'akei' meaning 'a thorn'), but our golden beauty is generally known as **'the wattle'**.

When the first huts were built in Sydney Cove, they used the well-known peasant form of construction of using horizontal saplings daubed on both sides with mud. This method of building was known as **'wattle-and-daub'**. Because most of the trees cut then were acacia saplings (there were stacks of them, and they were easy to cut!) our native plant has been known as the **'wattle'** ever since. There are several hundred species of **wattle**, most of which grow in Australia.

Aussie Outback ...

The remote part of Oz where 95% of the population don't live, but is visited largely by tourists who regard it as an adventure to go to the –

backblocks

back of beyond

back o' Bourke

beyond the Black Stump (non-existent place in remote outback). To be the best **'this side of the Black Stump'** is to have no equal.

Bullamakanka: backward, mythical place

bush: to **'go bush'** is to run away from civilization. The word **'bush'** came from the Dutch, 'bosch' through South African English.

Garn! Whaddyerthink this is – **Bush Week?** (you're having me on)

bushed: to get lost

donga: desolate area / dried-out watercourse / poor, temporary living quarters often for single males
to donga: loaf or bludge

middle of nowhere: anywhere outback

mulga: you could get **mulga madness** (become eccentric or insane) from living alone in the outback.

Gossip is passed along the **Mulga Wire** or **Bush Telegraph**.

Never Never: land from which you may never return

Woop-Woop: fictitious remote area where you may even find a **Woop-Woop pigeon** or **bushman's clock** (kookaburra)

> A whore in remote Oodnadatta
> Has a face total darkness can't flatter.
> Her clients don't care,
> 'Cos a woman's so rare
> That the looks of the hooker don't matter.

In 1919 a stockman, who was droving a herd of cattle outback, was joined at his camp one night by the rabbit-proof fence man.

He hadn't seen anyone for years, and was keen to catch up

on the news. During a lull in the conversation the stockman suddenly said, "By the way, we won the war, you know."

"That's good," said the rabbit-proof fence man. "I never did like them Boers."

Aussie Rules – The True Religion Of Oz!

The Irish gold-diggers started it all. They improvised a wild game which was something of a cross between hurling and Gaelic football. Thomas Wells and a friend decided to invent a new game, based on that developed by the diggers, to keep the Victorian cricketers in form during the winter. (Cricket is another religion instituted by the Brits and exported all over the world. Our greatest cricketing hero was Don Bradman or 'THE DON '.) The first game of **footie,** played in 1858 at Richmond Park, had forty players. It could last for days until the winning side scored two goals (if you belong to the Anti-Footie League, it seems as if things haven't changed much!). The rules were developed over the next 20 years or so, and the game gradually spread to all other states except New South Wales and Queensland. They probably resisted Aussie Rules because of its strong Victorian flavour – but they, too, have succumbed since the formation of the AFL!

"Up there, Cazaly!" (Roy Cazaly was a South Melbourne footie star in the 1920s and 1930s. The cry of encouragement has continued long past his time. The song, **'Up there, Cazaly!'** is sung along with each club's special anthem.

"Chewie on yer boot!" is a cry of **dis**couragement when the opposing team is set to kick a goal.

Aussie Salute ...

(the act of brushing away the flies from your face with your hand)

William Dampier started it all when in 1688 he described the old Oz as **'a land of sand, flies, and sore eyes'**.

I guess it's pretty logical that all the **blowies** or **butchers' canaries** should gather at the arse end of the world, but it can make you pretty aggro at times, especially at a barbie!

It's no wonder that we don't open our mouths when we speak. Our mothers told us, **"Remember, a shut mouth catches no flies."**

It is well-known that **Aussies will bet on anything – even two flies crawling up a wall.**

If there are **'no flies on *that* feller'** it means that he is shrewd or cunning.

Adults often told a child with freckles, **"There's no flies on you, but I can see where they've been"**.

If you are **'a fly in the ointment'** you are a real bother or problem.

If you **'have one with the flies'** or **'drink with the flies,'** you are drinking alone.

bar fly: habitual drinker at hotel bars

If you **'run around like a blue-arsed fly,'** you'll get nothing done.

fly-blown: broke or penniless

"You'd **make a blowfly sick!**"

The meal was **enough to put a blowfly off his tucker!**

Bit o' Bush Wisdom

**Some people are like flies –
They don't care if they hang around
Cow shit or lamingtons.**

"I don't like the flies in here," complained the diner.

"Well, come around tomorrow and we'll have some new ones," replied the waiter.

Aussies, State by State ...

New South Welshperson: Cornstalker – An obsolete term, but the lot from New South haven't earned themselves another alias. The next generation of Aussies after the arrival of the First Fleet in 1788 grew taller than their parents, and were described by the Poms in England as **'tall as stalks of corn'**, hence **'cornstalkers'**.

The Corner: area where borders of New South Wales, Queensland and South Australia meet

Northern Territorian: Top-Ender

Queenslander: Banana-Bender. Brissie is the capital city.

South Australian: Crow-Eater – South Oz suffered economically when its inhabitants joined the rush to the

Victorian goldfields in the mid 1800s and so those left were reduced to eating crow, a practice the Vics would like to see brought back when playing footie against them!

Tasmanian: Apple-Eater / Tassie Tiger

Victorian: Cabbage-Patcher (because of the size of the state), **Gum-Sucker** (because of habit of sucking gum balls plucked from acacia bushes), **Mexican** (New South lot refer to those living south of the border as such. Queenslanders regard those from New South Wales as **Mexicans**, too.)

West Australian: Sand-Groper (no shortage of sand in the west)

Four blokes were travelling in this car. One was a Tasmanian, one was a South Aussie, and there was a Queenslander and a Victorian.

Suddenly the Tasmanian opened his window and threw out apples.

"Why did you do that?" the others asked.

"Oh," said the Tasmanian, "I'm sick of the sight of apples. Everywhere I go in Tassie, it's apples, apples, apples."

A little later the South Aussie opened his window and threw out a couple of bottles of wine.

"Why did you do that?" asked the others.

"Oh," said the South Aussie, "everywhere I go in South Australia there's nothing but wine, wine, wine."

With that the Queenslander opened his window and threw out the Victorian!

An Australian in London was accosted by a lady of the night and invited around to her flat. He went with her, and she turned out to be a remarkable hostess. "I know what you boys like," she said. "How about a nice, hot pie with tomato sauce – just like you get at home?"

"You're kidding," said the Aussie.

She wasn't. "And some good, *cold* Australian bottled beer. How about that?"

The boy from Down Under could hardly believe his luck. He dealt with the pie and beer while she left to slip into something more comfortable. She reappeared a little later, wearing only a filmy robe.

"Now," she smiled, "come inside for some fun and games."

The Aussie stood up, grinning broadly. "Don't tell me you've even got a pool table?"

Great Australian Adjectives

Arse ...

The word **'arse'** originally meant 'the back end of an animal,' and was in normal, everyday use back in Pommie-land until about 1660. It was regarded as a swear word in Australia, but is coming back into everyday use again.

arse: buttocks / posterior also can mean 'good luck'

arse about: mess around

arse-about-face: back-to-front

arse from his elbow (wouldn't know): stupid

arse, get your ... into gear: get going / get organized

arse, get the: get the sack (get dismissed)

arse, give it the: throw out something

arse has dropped out of: failed

arsehole: despicable person

arsehole to breakfast: completely or totally

arse licker / arse kisser / crawl up one's arse: crawler / sycophant

arse off: to leave

arse out of his pants: poor

arse over tit: upside down

arse, talking through one's: ill-informed nonsense

arse up: a mess

arsey: unusually lucky

Great Australian Adjectives

as long as your arse points to the ground: while you're standing

baggy-arsed: rough

blow wind up his arse: flatter him

give someone the arse: send them packing

Kiss my arse! Go away, you annoy me!

more arse than class: more impudence than style

pain in the arse: a bore / nuisance

short arse: has duck's disease (tail's too close to the ground)

slack arse: lazy

smart arse: a know-all

so far up his arse I can see his shoelaces: conceited, inflated opinion of himself

sun shines out of his arse: can't do a thing wrong

tear-arse: wild, reckless, impulsive

tin-arse: lucky

Bastard ...

Knowing how to use this word is an essential part of being an Aussie. A relatively new Aussie we know proudly demonstrated how well he'd mastered the lingo by listing the various types of bastards. Although the word strictly means 'someone who is illegitimate' (from the word **'bast'**, which was the saddle used by French muleteers who often left 'pack-saddle children' – **'bastards'** – behind as they went from village to village), it has a unique application in Australia. By the way, sheilas are *never* bastards.

a bad bastard: you're frightened of him

a bastard from the bush: overbearing cadger

(not) a bad sort of bastard: you like him

a clever bastard: smart

a dirty bastard: lecherous

a dozey bastard: slow-witted, lazy

a lazy bastard: doesn't pull his weight

a lousy bastard: mean

a nasty bastard: untrustworthy

an officious bastard: over-asserts his authority

a poor bastard: you feel sorry for him

a queer bastard: doesn't conform / doesn't drink beer

a real bastard: you don't like him

a right bastard: you don't like him

a rotten bastard: you don't like him

a rude bastard: no manners – you don't like him

a stupid, bloody, mongrel bastard: you don't like him

a weak bastard: won't fight

that **bastard:** you don't like him

Y'old bastard! you *really* like him!

If you've had **a bastard of a day**, you're probably ready to jump down someone's throat and bark out his liver!

If you're **as happy as a bastard on Fathers' Day**, you're not exactly jumping over the moon, either!

An old cocky and his son had lived for many years on a broken-down farm when the son won $20,000 in a lottery. Overjoyed, the son picked out a dollar coin and gave it to his father.

The old chap looked at it and said drily, "I hope, son, you won't go throwing your money away like this. When I was young I was always careful. I never drank or gambled, and I was especially wary of women. As a matter of fact, I never ever married."

"Well, that's lovely, that is," said his son. "You know what that makes *me*, don't you?"

"Yes," replied his father, "and you're a greedy one, too!"

Bloody ...

Although indicating approval, it can be **bloody**-well-used any-**bloody**-where in a **bloody** sentence.

Originally from an old oath (By Our Lady), it was used by Protestants to stir up the Catholics who were loyal to the Virgin Mary. It was a major swear word until quite recently, due to the high proportion of **Rock Choppers** (RC's – Roman Catholics) in Australia. It is even used in advertisements now, e.g. "If you drink, then drive, you're **a bloody idiot!**"

Bloody hell!   **Bloody Nora!**   **Bloody oath!**

bloody-minded: stubborn, uncooperative

bloodsucker: one who borrows without paying back

blood's worth bottling: you're pretty good

Bugger ...

Another very old slur word, this time on the sexual habits of the Bulgarians. Although a well-known Australian swear word, **'bugger'** is now accepted in advertisements, too.

bugger about: to fool around

bugger-all: very little, nothing.

buggered: worn out

buggered if I know! Don't ask *me*!

buggerize about: behave ineffectually

buggerlugs / y'old bugger: affectionate term of endearment

Bugger me dead! exclamation of shock

Bugger it! Be buggered! Oh, bugger! curse

Bugger off! Go to buggery! Go away!

bugger up: cause damage to

funny / silly buggers: people who waste time on trivial things

like buggery: considerably, e.g. It stung like buggery!

off to buggery: a long way off course

If it's **a bugger of a day**, it could be because you got out the wrong side of the bed!

Great Australian Adjectives

Bull ...

rubbish, nonsense, uninformed

bull: e.g. "I think he's trying **to bull me**" (deceive, trick)

bull dust: claptrap — **bull dust** can also mean the fine dust on country roads

bull-headed: obstinate

bullshit: complete claptrap

bullshit artist: one who talks nonsense or exaggerates

bull's wool: exaggerated nonsense

charge like a wounded bull: charge excessive prices

cock and bull: nonsense, rubbish

doesn't know B from a bull's foot: stupid

get the bull by the horns: face up to a situation

like a bull at a gate: impatient

like a bull in a china shop: extremely clumsy, inept

within a bull's roar: anywhere near

Bit o' Bush Wisdom

Bullshit
Baffles
Brains

A young city bloke inherited a cattle station. He wasn't there long before he realized his cattle were being stolen in large numbers, and it was obvious that the cattle duffer was his neighbour. When he discussed the matter with a local he was told, "Be careful. He's a tough bastard. He'll shoot you as quick as look at you if you accuse him of pinching your steers."

So the young bloke thought for a bit, and then wrote his neighbour a letter ending with ... 'and I'd appreciate it if you'd refrain from leaving your branding iron where my foolish cattle can sit on it.'

Blokes, Jokers, Sheilas And Skirts

CHILDREN — **ankle biters / beggars / billy lids / brats / horrors / kids / kiddiewinks / little buggers / vegemites / littlies / nippers / pipsqueaks / rug-rats / shavers / terrors / tin lids / tykes / whippersnappers / young-uns**

WIFE — **ball and chain / battle-axe / cheese 'n kisses / hair brush / missus old lady / trouble and strife / war department**

battler (little Aussie) ordinary working man trying to make a living against overwhelming odds

black sheep: failure / outcast / disreputable member of family

boofhead: stupid person, often a friendly insult. **'Boofhead'** was the name of a comic strip character in the 1940s. Maybe came from English dialect 'bufflehead,' meaning 'bullock head.'

bloke: a man. Thought to have come from a gypsy language, meaning 'a man.' In English it was used for a man who was in a position of authority, but in Australia it became a generalized term for any man. To be regarded as **'a good bloke'** is the highest form of praise among Aussie men. The modern word 'guy' does not have quite the same meaning.

blood'n blister (r.s.) sister

blow-in: a new-comer / someone who arrives unexpectedly

boss cocky: one in charge

bruiser: bully, tough person

bunny: fall guy, fool

bush lawyer: one who gives unqualified advice – probably has the gift of the gab and the ability to sound convincing.

bushwacker: someone who comes from a rural area and / or acts like it

butterfingers: someone who continually drops things

china plate (me ol' china) (r.s.) mate

chook: old woman **'nice old chook'** **'silly old chook'**

codger: fellow – odd or eccentric / mean or miserly

conchie: over conscientious

couch potato: lazy, one who sits and watches television all day

cove: a man. Like 'bloke', it originally meant 'someone in charge'.

cream-puff: effeminate / cowardly / physically weak

crumpet (bit of) woman regarded as sex object

dag: amusing / awkward / eccentric / odd / unfashionable / scruffy. Although 'a dag' is strictly the substance (crap) hanging from a sheep's bum, we affectionately refer to someone as **'a bit of a dag.'**

deadhead: dull, good-for-nothing

dero: alcoholic vagrant

digger: cobber, mate first used on the gold diggings for the men of the Eureka Stockade at Ballarat. Then it was applied to the Anzac infantrymen during World War 1 because they believed their main job was to dig trenches. Now it can mean any soldier, or just an affectionate term of address.

dingaling: silly, amusing

dingbat: eccentric

dingo: cowardly, treacherous – like our native dog, the dingo

dobber: an informer. Aussies have a reluctance to 'dob' anyone into someone in a position of authority. If you 'dob' someone in you're 'a right bastard.'

dole bludger: someone who is content to live off social security

dope: stupid

drack-sack: dowdy woman

drongo: a born loser / complete idiot. **Drongo** was a racehorse from the 1920s who never won a race.

drop-kick: useless person

dry character: humorous, but in an unemotional, impersonal way

duffer: foolish, incompetent person probably came from Scottish 'duffar' meaning stupid, inactive person

dyke: a lesbian (from American 'dike' – to 'dress up'), in this case, 'to dress up like a man'

earbasher: someone who talks incessantly / a bore

earwig: eavesdropper / stickybeak

fizzgig: police informer, but more often someone whose name you can't recall e.g. "Remember old fizzgig who lived next door to us in Woop-Woop?"

galah: fool / idiot hard to say why we attribute stupidity to the pink and grey birds – maybe it's because they chatter so much. The outback radio time for private conversation is called **"a galah session"**.

galoot: stupid / awkward / clumsy

gasbag: incessant talker / gossip

good looker / good sort / top sort: attractive person – usually applies to females

greaser / brown noser: flatterer, obsequious person

greenie: conservationist

grizzle-guts: complains or whinges constantly

hard case: witty / amusing / tough / cynical

hoon: lout / fast, reckless driver

hot-shot: sarcastic term for someone proficient

humdinger: remarkable person

illywhacker: small-time confidence trickster – anyone with a come-on spiel is said **'to whack the illy'**

jail-bait: girl or boy under the legal age of consent for sex

Joe Blow: average man in the street

joker: a bloke

kook: harmless eccentric

lair: flashily dressed show-off a **mug lair** is both vulgar and stupid

'to lairise' is to show off in order to get attention

larrikin: lout / hoodlum / little regard for authority from a Worcestershire dialect meaning 'mischievous and frolicsome youth' — **'a bit of a larrikin'** is someone often admired for his daring exploits

left-footer: a Roman Catholic

local yokel: well-known resident of a town, suburb, etc.

mate / cobber / sport: friend. 'Mates' were men who worked as partners in jobs that were almost impossible to do alone, who went to war together, supported each other, and usually drank together.

No matter what happens, a man must **'stick by his mates.'**

Also used loosely when addressing acquaintances and strangers –

"G'day, mate!" "Goodonya, mate!" "Howyagoin, mate?" "Righto, mate!" "Seeya, mate!"

However, it can also be used to indicate hostility, e.g. **"I'll fix *you*, mate!"**

'Sport' is also a familiar form of address, sometimes indicating hostility as well, e.g. **"Listen here, sport!"** However, if you're **'a good sport'**, you're amicable, easy-going, honest and generous. If you're urged to **'be a sport,'** it is hoped that you'll help someone or act in a reasonable manner.

melon: stupid / fool

misery guts: constant complainer / whinger

mug: a bloke who hasn't a clue / beginner / sucker

muggins: person with no mind of his own

mutt: stupid (shortened from **'mutton head'**)

new chum: novice

no-hoper: incompetent / social misfit

nong: idiot / simple-minded – from Yorkshire dialect 'ning-nang', meaning a worthless or troublesome person

ocker: beer-swilling / boorish / ignorant / loud – from a character in the 1960s programme, 'The Mavis Brampston Show'

old boy / old geeser / old man: old man / husband / father

old cheese / old dear / old girl / old woman: old woman / wife / mother

old cow / old crow: disliked woman

old fogey: boringly conservative in ideas and methods

old grouch: bad-tempered / constantly complaining

old timer: old person, especially an old man

oldies: parents or in-laws

piker: someone who opts out of an agreement / gives up easily

pissant: game / courageous

poofter: derogatory term for homosexual

Pommy: English person – from rhyming slang for an **'immigrant'** in the 1800s. By the 1900s it had become 'pommygrant' or 'pommygranates', which was then shortened to **'Pommies.'**

prick teaser: woman who refuses to have sex with a man after leading him on to expect it

quandong: woman who refuses to have sex after being wined and dined

quince / shirt-lifter: male homosexual

rat / ratfink: despicable, untrustworthy person

ratbag: rogue / eccentric – from old expression 'to get rats' or wild ideas

rev-head: fast driver of a car or motorbike

scab: non-union worker / mean / contemptible / disloyal

septic tank / seppo: Yank (r.s.)

Sheila: / Charlie Wheeler (r.s.) young woman, girlfriend. So many Irish females were named after the Celtic goddess of fertility that **'Sheila'** came to mean any female, Irish or not. This use of **'sheila'** was brought to Oz by the English.

shithead: worthless / mean / stupid

skirt (bit or piece of) a woman considered as a sex object

skite: one who boasts or brags

slime-ball: repulsive, obsequious person

spanner: girl who really 'turns men on' sexually

sponger: free-loader, one who lives at the expense of others

suckhole: ingratiating, obsequious person

sundowner: swagman / tramp who arrived at sundown when it was too late to do any work in exchange for food and shelter.

swagman: carried his swag as he walked around the country, living off earnings from occasional jobs or gifts of food or money.

top-off: an informer

top-of-the-wozzer: number one man

wacker: crazy / eccentric / sometimes amusing

wally: idiot

wanker: self-deluding idiot

warb: unkept / useless

wet: weak **wet behind the ears:** naïve

wet blanket: pessimist / one who dampens enthusiasm

yobbo: lout / slob

Bit o' Bush Wisdom

**Keep a grin on your mug
When things are down,
And you'll always have
True mates around.**

**True mates are like dogs;
Some are pedigrees,
Some are mongrels,
But they'll always come when you need them.**

A fly-by-night character applied for a job at a Queensland cattle station. He began skiting to the boss about his riding ability.

"Alright," said the boss, "I'll give you a try-out." He called for Bindi-eye Jack – a fair to average bucker – to be saddled.

"Think y' can stick him?" he asked the blatherskite.

"Ride 'im till sundown – ride 'im till the stars come out!" bragged the big mouth. He mounted Bindi-eye Jack, which immediately threw him so high in the air that he landed flat on his back in the dust several yards away.

"Huh!" said the boss, turning on his heel, "That was a bloody short day!"

Body Language

"I'm no oil painting, but I scrub up alright."

Parts of the body beautiful:

BUTTOCKS — acre / arse / backside / bazooka / bottle-and-glass (r.s.) bum / buns / butt / cheeks / Khyber Pass (r.s.) seat / sit-me-down beam / bottie / bronze / bum / buns / cheeks, / jacksy

> **three axe handles wide across the beam** (very big bottom)
> **'bum to mum'** was an order for footie players to abstain from sexual activity on the eve of a match
> to **give a bum steer** is to mislead

PENIS — Alec the phallic / cock / dagger / dick / dipstick / donger / donk / doodle / ferret / Hoffman brick (r.s.) knob / love muscle / meat / member / mutton / old man, bloke, feller / one-eyed trouser snake / pecker / percy / pizzle / pork sword / prick / prong / pud / rod / roger / sausage / short arm / tassle / third leg / tommy / tossle / vital organ / wedding tackle / whistle / wick / wife's best friend / willie / zubrick

a **clever dick** is a know-all a **dickhead** is a fool or idiot

dipstick can also be an insult, e.g. "G'day, **Dipstick!**"

FRECKLES — **angel kisses / fly poo**

A.P.C. (Arm Pits and Crutch), **budgie bath** / **Effie, Tessie and Bessie** (Face, Tits and Bum), **Four F's** (Face, Fungi, Fanny and Feet), **Mary Pickford in Three Acts** (face, feet and genitals), **possible bath** (up and down as far as possible, and leave **'possible'** until later), **Queen Elizabeth bath** (just a dash of powder), **sparrow bath** (a dip and a flap under the wings), **whore's bath** (quick rinse of the genitals.) These are all terms invented by women to describe quick washes on non-bath days. Bath night was once a week, usually on Saturday (the going-out night.)

BREASTS — **apples / big brown eyes / boobs / boozies / boulders / bumpers / charlies / choozies / fried eggs / fun bags / headlights / jugs / knockers / melons / norks / nubbies / num nums / tits /**
'norks' – from NORCO, a New South Wales dairy – logo was a cow with big udders
She's got T.B. (Two Beauts)

ANUS — **arsehole / blurter / brown-eye / bumhole / date / dead-eye / freckle / dinger / North Pole (r.s.) ort / quoit / ring**
to **'chuck a browneye'** – to bend over and bare your bottom

HEAD — **attic / block / book / coconut / crust of bread (r.s.) dome / load / noggin / noodle / nut / pimple / scone / top storey**

BELLY, STOMACH — **Auntie Nellie / bingie / Ned Kelly (r.s.)**

EYES — **baby blues / headlights / mince pies (r.s.) optics / peepers**
a **shiner:** black eye **luggage:** bags under the eyes
butcher's hook / Captain Cook (r.s.) a look
If looks could kill, you'd be dead long ago!

LEGS — **bacon and eggs (r.s.) drivers / drumsticks / gams / Ginger Meggs, pegs (r.s.) pins / stumps / timbers:** to go by **shank's pony** is to walk
legs all the way to heaven (long and lovely)
Bet I know what she puts behind her ears to attract men – her legs!

Body Language

TESTICLES — balls / bollocks / cods / crown jewels / gonads / goolies / Kanakas, knackers / marbles / niagras (r.s. for Niagra Falls) orchestras (r.s. for orchestra stalls),
got him **by the balls** (in one's power)
Hope y' **balls** turn into bicycle wheels and pedal up y' arse!
balls-up: a blunder, chaotic He's **got balls** (courage)
ball-tearer: He's great! Terrific!

NOSE — beak / bugle / conk / honker / hooter / horn / I suppose (r.s.) Lionel Rose (r.s.) schnoz / schnozzle (Yiddish) snoot / snout:

beer gut: PROTRUDING BELLY in males. He's got **a verandah over the toy box / play station**

bell ringer / onkaparinga (r.s.) FINGER
fingernails in mourning: dirty fingernails

NAKED — birthday suit / bollocky / buff / nuddy / raw /
starkers. standing **in the bollocky / in the raw**

BODY — bod / chassis / shaft:

VAGINA —box / daisy / fanny / front bum / honey pot / mickey / muff / pussy / snatch / twat / quim
daisy was a Victorian word which may explain the popularity of the song of that era, 'Daisy, Daisy!'

SNEEZE —bread and cheese (r.s.)
The custom of saying **"God bless you!"** when someone sneezed dates back to the Middle Ages when it was thought that a sneeze left an opening in one's head where the Devil could slip through into someone's mind. Thus "God bless you!" was a polite way of telling the Devil to rack off!

bumfluff: first growth of FACIAL HAIR on a young man's face

PREGNANT — **bun in the oven, in pod, in the pudding club / preggers / preg / up the duff / up the spout:** In modern military slang, **'one up the spout'** means that a firearm has a bullet in the breach, ready for firing – get the similarity of the situation?
Vatican roulette: rhythm method of contraception – so unreliable that one could be **in the pudding club** in no time at all! Maybe she *should* have danced all night! If a woman had an illegitimate baby, it was often described as just **a fart in a bonnet.**

bottle blonde: woman with DYED HAIR

bushfire blonde: woman with RED HAIR

suicide blonde: DYED by her own hand?

to **get in someone's hair** (annoy them)

Keep your hair on! (Keep calm)

let your hair down (behave in an uninhibited manner)

put hair on your chest (keep you fit)

without turning a hair (showing no emotion)

MOUTH — **cake hole / chops / gob / kisser / north-and-south(r.s.) / trap**

FACE — **Chevy Chase (r.s.) dial / mush / pan / phiz / phizzog / puss / smiler**

fish-face   poker-face   sour-puss

comic cuts: GUTS

come a gutser (fall) **gutsy** (daring, brave)

had a gutsful (fed up with)

haven't got the guts (nerve)

Body Language

have (someone's) guts for garters (get revenge)

hate (someone's) guts rough as guts

spill your guts (give information)

crap / jobbies / number twos / poo / shit: EXCREMENT

'Crap' used to refer to the dregs in a wine barrel, but became linked to excretory functions through cistern manufacturer, Thomas Crapper.

Cut the crap! (Stop talking nonsense!)

in the poo (in trouble)

put shit on (criticize)

up shit creek (in big trouble)

to **shit in one's nest** (to ruin one's own circumstances)

shit on the liver – S.O.L. (bad-tempered, irritable)

Dad and Dave (r.s.) SHAVE

dooks / hooks / maulers / mitts / paws: HANDS

molly-dooker: left-handed

"Put up your **dooks** and fight!"

Errol Flynn / Gunga Din (r.s.) CHIN

face fungus: BEARD / MOUSTACHE

soup strainer: MOUSTACHE

Farmer Giles (r.s.) PILES or HAEMORRHOIDS

cure for piles – **bare your bum near an angry dog!**

fart / hum / jam tart (r.s.) let off / parachute / make a smelly / step on a duck / unload: BREAK WIND via the anus

fart-arse: to waste time

fart-sack: bed, sleeping bag

farts at both ends: loud-mouthed bore

organ-arse: farts audibly **stupid, old fart**

A **fart** is a fool who has lost a good home.

> A **fart** is such a useful thing,
> It gives the body ease;
> It warms the bed on winter nights,
> And chloroforms the fleas.
> Wherever you be,
> Let the wind go free.

fat / hard-on / horn / stiff: an ERECTION

to **crack a fat** is to attain an erection

MENSTRUATION – **flag / flowers / girls' week / monthlies / rags / visitor**
    hang the flags out / in the flowers / got the rags / beetroot sandwiches / little white mice or fruit cocktails (tampons) / **manhole covers / white bread** –
    all Sheila-speak for menstruation and applications

EARS – **flaps / lugholes / lugs / wing nuts / Williamstown Piers (r.s.):**

TONGUE – **flap strap**

CONDOM — frenchie / frog / little rain at / nosebag
wearing a condom — **like having a shower with a raincoat on**

contraceptive for men — **put it in their shoes, and it makes them limp**

contraceptive for women — **aspro between the knees**

contraception advice: '**Take advice from one who knows, Tie your nightie to your toes.**'

BUT — '**if you want a little boy, pull down the blind.**'

ELBOW — **funny bone**
a pun on the name of the bone which runs from the shoulder to the elbow, the 'humerus'

NECK — **Gregory Peck / bushel and peck (r.s.)**

PIDDLE — **Hey diddle diddle / Jimmy Riddle / Nelson Riddle (r.s.) / drain the dragon / flash Fanny at the Fowlers** (Fowlers was a company who made toilet pans) **flog the lizard / go to the bathroom / go to the little girls' room / go for a snake's hiss (r.s.) go for a you'n me (r.s.) / have a twinkle / powder one's nose / see a man about a dog / shake hands with the vicar or wife's best friend / splash one's boots / siphon the python / take one's dog for a walk / water the horse / unbutton the mutton**

The end result of a shock or laughing fit may be that you **piddle yourself** or **wet yourself.**

SKIN — **hide / pelt**

BOIL — **Conan Doyle (r.s.)**

PIMPLE — **goob / wopty-gobble / zit**

PISS (urine) — **hit and miss / Johnny Bliss (r.s.) all piss and wind** (empty talk)

pissing down (raining heavily)
piss in someone's pocket (being sycophantic)
piss in the wind (attempt something futile)

piss someone off (send them away)

JAW — **jackdaw / rabbit's paw (r.s.)**

MASTURBATE — **ack off / pull the pud / wank / whack off / whipping the dripping**
Mrs Palmer and her five daughters (hand) – useful aid
play pocket billiards (play with genitals via trouser pockets)
wet dream (an exciting dream resulting in ejaculation)

DIARRHOEA — **Jimmy Britts / tom tits (r.s.) / trots**
have the shits (be annoyed) **in the shit** (in trouble)

DEFECATE — **do one's business / lay a cable / relieve oneself**
shit for brains (stupid)
shit stirrer (trouble maker)

CLITORIS — **little man in the boat / button / clit / joy buzzer**

love handles CELLULITE (spare tyres)

ta-ta flaps: loose skin hanging from upper arms

map of Tassie: (female) PUBIC AREA

FEET — **mud flaps / plates of meat (r.s.) puppies / trotters:**

SEXUAL INTERCOURSE — **naughty / nookie / poke / quickie (quick one) / root / screw / shag:**

naughty bits: GENITALS
hung like a horse (well-endowed in the genital department)

outie: protruding NAVEL– opposite to an **innie**

Body Language

TEETH — **pearlies / pearly gates / choppers / clackers / eating tackle, Hampsteads (r.s. for Hampstead Heath) pegs**
falsies / graveyard chompers: FALSE TEETH
Early dentures were made with springs until an American dentist discovered that suction would keep them in place. For a time other people's teeth were fastened to a plate, and so the poor often sold their teeth. There was a thriving trade in teeth from the dead as well.

as scarce as hen's teeth (very rare)

piece de resistance: CONSTIPATION

PUBIC HAIR — **pubes / short and curlies / wool**
got him by the short and curlies (in one's power)

HEART — **pump / ticker:**

randy / ranji: SEXUALLY EXCITED
randy as a bitch on heat / drover's dog / mallee bull

MUCUS — **snot / dewdrops:**
boogies / goobies / goolies; HARDENED MUCUS

spunk: SEMEN

Warwick Farms (r.s.) - or just **Warwicks:** ARMS

Checkin' Out the Bodywork ...

ball of muscle: fit

brown as a berry: very suntanned – not so fashionable since the 'Slip-Slop-Slap' campaigns

buff / stacked: well built

Face

Don't pull a face like that – the wind'll change and you'll stay like it!

a good pair of corned beef grabbers (protruding teeth)

a mean dog that barks behind a hedge (thick beard)

a rat looking over a straw broom (bearded)

egg-shell blonde (bald)

like a chook's bum

like a deformed mallee root

like a festered pickle bottle (acne)

like a gummy shark (toothless)

like a lumpy rice pudding (acne)

like a Newcastle docker (ugly)

like a road map / run over jam tins / the back end of a smashed tram (damned ugly!)

like a robber's dog

like a stopped clock

like the wild man of Borneo

more chins than a Chinese laundry

mouth like a parrot's arsehole

so hard you could crack rocks on it

that would fight a bulldog

as ugly as a hat full of arseholes / bums

Large ...

built like a brick shithouse

built like the side of a house

Body Language

Looks Like ...

a birch broom in a fit

a bunch of cocky feathers (dressed up)

a Chinese brothel on a Sunday morning (dirty, untidy)

a crow staring down a pickle bottle

a drowned rat (wet, bedraggled)

a drover's bitch – all tits and teeth

death warmed up

mutton dressed up as lamb (older woman dressed in clothing much too young in style)

seen better heads on a glass of beer

sight for sore eyes (pretty good)

something the cat dragged in

So Short ...

he had duck's disease (bum too close to the ground)

he was knee-high to a grasshopper

So Tall ...

he was like two yards of pump water

So Thin:

he was like a bag of soup bones

he was like a bottle of milk with shoes on

he was as skinny as a bean pole

he was as skinny as a chicken's instep

he was as skinny as a Nullarbor rabbit

he was as skinny as a rake

he was as skinny as a walking hairpin

he was like a fart with the shit scraped off

if she turned side on, she'd slip through a crack in the floor-boards

he could stand in the shade of a crowbar

he had to run around in the shower to get wet

he was like a match with the wood scraped off

he wouldn't cast a shadow

So Wide ...

she was like a taxi with four doors open, and her chassis needed tightening

she was twice around the gasworks

Ruminating Riddle

What is a well-proportioned girl?
One with a narrow waist and a broad mind.

Bit o' Bush Wisdom

No-one gets a tin arse
By sitting on it.

Body Language

An English couple were returning home from a holiday in America, and they decided to try to smuggle in a rare snake and a skunk. "I'll wear the snake around my waist as a belt," said the husband. "You can put the skunk down your knickers."

"But," protested the wife, "what about the smell?"

Her husband shrugged. "If it dies, it dies."

Bouquets – givin' a pat on th' back

YOU'RE: **a bit of all right!**

a bobby-dazzler (from Yorkshire dialect – a 'dazzler' means someone or something of striking merit)

a corker!

a little beauty!

a little bottler!

a little champion!

a little humdinger!

a little ripsnorter!

a little trimmer!

Goodonya!

just the bee's knees!

one out of the box!

pure merino!

top-notch!

worth your weight in cocky chaff / gold

Brickbats – or stickin' th' boots in

couldn't get a root in a brothel with a $100 note

couldn't get a root in a woodyard

couldn't run guts for a slow butcher

If arseholes could fly, this place would be an airport.

If you pick your nose, your head'll cave in.

Men are like toilets – either engaged or full of shit.

not worth a pinch of cocky's poop

so low you could walk under a snake's belly without ducking your head

You'd give a dog's arse heartburn!

You're as green as you are cabbage-looking.

You're lower than a snake's armpit!

Ruminating Riddle

What tool grows sharper with use?
The tongue.

A woman who was reading an article on life expectancy turned to the man beside her and said, "Do you know that every time I breathe, someone dies?"

"Have you ever tried mouthwash?" asked the man.

Clobber: Gettin' Y' Gear On

"I haven't got a thing to wear!"
"Well, paint your bum black and go naked!"

If you're DRESSED IN YOUR BEST CLOTHES, you're:

all dolled up

all laired up

done up in one's best bib and tucker (bibs and tuckers were worn to protect clothing in 17th century)

done up like a Christmas tree

done up like a dinner

done up like a pox-doctor's clerk

done up like a sore toe

done up like an old moll at a christening

done up to the nines

dressed fit to kill

dressed in one's fancy duds

dressed in one's glad rags

dressed in one's Sunday best

dressed to beat the band

pooned up

flash as a rat with a gold tooth

spivved up

spruced up

Clobber: Gettin' Y' Gear On

Gear (or Clobber)

akubra: wide-brimmed felt hat, so-called because of an early manufacturer's brand name

bag of fruit (r.s.) suit

bathers / cossies / Speedos (from early brand name), **swimmers, togs:** bathing costume (word used varies between states)

beanie: close-fitting knitted cap

bloomers / knickers / panties / scanties: women's underpants

boob-tube: women's elasticised summer top

booties: knitted baby's shoes

bra / harness / over-shoulder-boulder-holder / sling-shot: brassiere

baggies (baggy trousers) **britches / cords** (corduroy) **daks / duds / pants / poop-catchers** (loose-fitting, ankle-tight) / **stove-pipes** (tight-fitting) / **strides / tweeds:** trousers

brothel boots: / sneakers: soft-soled shoes

brunch coat: women's light dressing-gown

bushman's hanky: sleeve

nose rag: hanky

cardie: cardigan

civvies: ordinary clothes – not a uniform

clod-hoppers: shoes or boots

Darwin pyjamas: no pyjamas

flatties: women's flat-heeled shoes **middies:** low-heeled shoes

wedgies: wedge-shaped heels

grundies / Reginalds – short for **Reginald Grundies (r.s.) G-string** (minimal genital covering) **nut-chokers / under-chunders underdaks / undies / Y-fronts:** men's underpants

gummies / wellies: gumboots

hotpants: sexy shorts for women

Jackie Howe: black or navy woollen work singlet worn by labourers – from name of champion shearer

jam-jars: thick-lensed spectacles

Japanese safety shoes: thongs

jarmies / PJ's: pyjamas

long johns: men's long underwear

mockies: moccasins (worn predominantly by Victorians)

monkey suit: dinner suit / suit with tie

pinny: apron

roll-ons / step-ins: women's control briefs

runners: sandshoes

slip: petticoat

sloppy joe: loose-fitting jumper

slouch hat: Australian army hat Originally, the **slouch hat** was turned up on the right side to prevent it being pushed off during rifle drill. Since the Boer War, the hat has been turned up on the left, where it remains. A very early meaning of **'slouch'** was to 'hang' or 'droop'. Because a brim should turn down then, not up, on a **'slouch'** hat, you could say the term was a bit of a 'cock-up.'

Clobber: Gettin' Y' Gear On

tank top: resembling a singlet

titfer (r.s.) a hat ('tit fer tat')

twin-set: matching jumper and cardigan

ug boot: fleecy-lined, sheepskin boot

wig warmer: hat

winkle-pickers: pointed-toe shoes

woollies: warm, woollen clothing

Bit o' Bush Wisdom

**Put your strides on before your boots
Or you could land on your face.**

**There was a young man from Tuncurry,
Who went out of his house in a hurry.
He'd left off his pants,
Got bitten by ants,
And was last seen waist-deep in the Murray.**

"That's a nice suit you're wearing? Who went for the fitting?"

"I always dress to please my husband – I make each dress last at least ten years."

Sue: "I always know what to do to cheer myself up. Whenever I'm down in the dumps, I get myself some new clothes."

Sally: "I always wondered where you got them from!"

Dead as a Maggot

been carried out feet first

cashed in his / her chips (if you've lost all your chips when gambling, you've lost all your money)

caught it

clagged the bag

conked

creamed

croaked

curled up his / her toes

dead and buried

dead as a dodo

dead as a doornail (medieval doors were studded with large-headed nails which were struck by the knocker. After being pounded constantly, the nails would be definitely 'dead.'

done for

dusted

given up the ghost

gone / a goner

gone west: Because the setting sun signals the end of the day, it was thought that the west was the home of departed spirits. Near the western gate in the wall surrounding the city of London, was Newgate Prison. The trip to the gallows, often after being paraded through the city streets, was therefore **'going west.'**

had it

had the dick / had the Richard

had the gong

had the sword

history

kaput

keeled over

kicked off

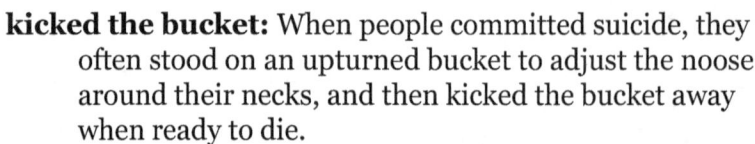

kicked the bucket: When people committed suicide, they often stood on an upturned bucket to adjust the noose around their necks, and then kicked the bucket away when ready to die.
Slaughtered animals were suspended from a wooden frame called a 'bucket' – in dying they often **'kicked the bucket.'**

passed away

passed in his / her marble tossed in his / her alley

pegged out

popped off

pushing up daisies

rat-shit

rooted

six foot under

snapped his / her twig

snuffed it

stone cold

stuffed

turned up his / her toes

If you **kill someone** you: -

bump them off / do away with them / do them in / knock them off rub them out / wipe them out

Did You Know?

Before medical practices made it possible to ascertain exactly when someone breathed his / her last, people were sometimes buried alive. Some bright spark hit on the idea of putting a rope in the coffin of the dear departed. The rope was attached to a bell, which could then be used to signal the fact that there was still a bit of life left in the old bugger, and he / she could be rescued. From this practice came the expression **'saved by the bell'**.

The custom of **wearing black for mourning** is a pagan one. People wore black as a disguise so that the ghost of the deceased might not recognize them and start haunting them (maybe the idea stemmed from the death of a mother-in-law!) It was also thought to confuse any demons who might be hangin' about lookin' for more lives to snatch. It became a sign of someone's sad state of mind, and was a signal for friends to avoid subjects which might distress a mourner.

The invention of **coffins** was more to do with keeping the departed at arm's distance from the living than for propriety. People were desperate to keep the dead person from returning and becoming a **'creepygogotcha'** to the living. Sometimes the scone (head) was cut off and put between the pegs (legs). Nailing down the coffin, or using stone coffins were added precautions. The **tombstone** was also a way of holding the dead down under the sod, and **cemeteries** were originally fields to protect the living from being contaminated by those who were **'six foot under'**.

'Hearse' was the French word for 'harrow.' In the 13th century, peasants found that by inverting their farm harrow, it became a giant candlestick and was carried to the church in a funeral procession. It gradually was made large enough to carry the coffin to the church as well. Wheels were added in order to carry the coffin to the grave, and later horses pulled this 'wagon.' Then the horse-drawn wagon was replaced by a motorized wagon – to become known as a **'hearse.'**

The old farmer was on his death-bed. He beckoned his long-suffering wife and said, "Dearest, you were with me during the Great Depression."

She dabbed at a tear running down her cheek.

"You were with me through all of those droughts."

She sobbed silently.

"You were with me when we lost the place in the bushfire. You were with me when the cattle prices crashed, and the wool prices collapsed, and you're here when I'm about to kick the bucket."

The woman was openly sobbing.

The farmer continued, "Y'know, I'm beginning to think you've brought me nothing but bad luck!"

>
> **Poor old Nelly's dead,**
> **She died last night in bed.**
> **They put her in a coffin.**
> **She fell right out the bottom.**

Dunnies: An Aussie Icon

Hope y' chooks turn into emus, and kick y' dunny door down!

'Dunny' comes from an English dialect, 'dunneken;' 'dunne' means 'dung' and 'ken' is a 'house' – therefore, 'a dung' or 'shit house.'

The Aussie dunny has long been a feature of the Australian landscape. In the country it was often a 'long-drop' – usually erected some distance from the house because of the flies and the smell

(all alone like a country dunny.) There weren't too many dunnies that were **'so flash it'd make your fanny look shabby!'**

After a Monday washday, Mum would toss the embers from under the copper down our long-drop to burn the paper and skedaddle the red-backs **(a red-back on the toilet seat** was *not* just a myth!) The embers did their job, but the after-smell was definitely **'on the nose!'** Occasionally, she would accidentally set the timber frame of the dunny alight, and it was all hands on deck to save the dunny from 'ex-stinkshon!' Never saw any Joe Blakes(snakes) in our thunder box – obviously the smell made them steer clear of the sh'ouse!

Recycled newspaper (cut into hanky-size pieces for use as dunny paper) was hung on a spike of wire or a large safety-pin inside the dunny within reach of the sitter. It was a source of frustration when the paper cutter cut through the latest episode of 'The Phantom' or 'Bluey and Curley!'

There was always at least one member of the family who was afflicted with **'Dishes Diarrhoea'** – they always seemed to head for the **throne** at dish-washing time.

Once in a while a new hole had to be dug, the building moved to sit over top of the hole, and the old hole filled over. 'Course,

you needed to mark the spot so that Bluey didn't bury his bone there for a while.

When New Year's Eve pranks were popular, my uncles moved the family dunny to a spot behind a wormwood bush. Their old man was not amused when, after a night of too much salami and plonk, he tried to locate the dunny next morning.

Another common trick was to lob a couple of rocks on the dunny's roof – it certainly upset the occupant's concentration!

Because the dunny was always installed some distance from the house, it was common to have a **'gazunder'**, **'thunder mug'** or **'po'** under the bed in order to avoid the hazardous trip to the outside dunny during the night. One could **'reign over China'** instead!

Label on a gazunder: -

> **Wash me out and keep me clean,**
> **And I won't tell what I have seen!**

The townies had the convenience of a night-cart man (san-man) who removed the dunny can (positioned under the dunny seat) each week. It was an advantage if the dunny was unoccupied at the time of collection, despite the can being removed by way of a small door at the rear of the little 'ouse. Dunny cans were often carried on the san-man's head (**as flat as a shit-carter's hat**), and stories of rusted cans, and retrieval of valuable objects from the cans were common.

The little door at the rear of the dunny provided convenient access for pranksters to startle an occupant with a well-aimed feather or switch of gum leaves!

During World War I, sanitary and water carts were built by the foundry of John Furphy, at Shepparton in Victoria. **'A furphy'** became known as 'a rumour', as many stories were told and passed on as the water or sanitary cart (bearing the Furphy name), did the rounds of the troops.

In Australia a **LAVATORY** is a / an:

Aunt Mary
bog
crap-house
diddy

dunny (a **dunny budgie** is a blow-fly)
dyke / Vandyke / Vandy
Gene Tunny (r.s.)
jakes
la la
lav / lavvy
little girl's room
loo
parliament (where one sits)
perky pan

piss-house
pissaphone (army urinal made with funnel)
poet's corner
powder room (women's toilet)
pussy palace (women only)
reading room
shithouse / sh'ouse
summer house (some are f' men, some are f' women)
throne
throttling pit (urinal)
thunder box / toilie / toot
twinkle palace

It wasn't considered genteel to tell companions that you were going to the lavatory / dunny, etc., and so it was common to **'flash fanny at the Fowlers'** (Fowlers was a well-known brand of toilet pan),

'go for a twinkle', 'go off to see the wizard,' 'go where all the nobs hang out,' 'kill a snake,' 'pay a visit,' 'point Percy at the porcelain,' 'shake hands with the wife's best friend' or 'unemployed male,' 'spend a penny,' or **'splash one's boots.'**

To **'kangaroo in the loo,'** you perch over a lavatory seat to avoid sitting on it.

A **'thumber'** is a measurement made with the thumb (when visiting the sh'ouse at night) to ascertain the amount of room left in the lavatory can – bet you're glad the flush-loo was invented!

A **'tote ticket'** or **'pakapoo ticket'** is toilet paper

Boys were instructed by their mothers (in the interests of cleanliness) to **'put their apparatus right in the pan.'**

On the dunny door ...

Because a part of everyone's day is spent in the dunny, it is a place where poets and philosophers alike can exercise their wit.

**Do not stand upon the seat,
The crabs here jump fifteen feet!
If you sprinkle when you twinkle,
Be a sweetie, wipe the seatie.**

**Here I sits broken-hearted,
Paid my penny, but only farted.**

**It's better to fart and stink a little
Than bust your arse and be a cripple.**

Dunnies feature in countless colloquialisms –

as full as a seaside dunny on Boxing Day

cunning as a shithouse rat

bangs like a dunny door in a gale

as strong as a night-cart in a heatwave

The Two Dunnies

We once had two dunnies outside,
But mother fell down one and died,
My uncle, her brother,
Then fell down the other,
And now they're interred side by side.

Ruminating Riddle

Who is the strongest man in town?
The night-cart man
He can carry what everyone else has to drop.

Exclamations: Amazement and Disbelief

Amazement:

Blimey Charlie!

Bloody Hell!

Bloody Nora!

Bloody oath!

Blow me down!

Boy-oh-boy!

Brother!

Bugger-me-dead!

By cripes!

By gum!

By jove!

Can you beat that!

Christ almighty!

Cor!

Crikey!

Cripes!

Cut me down and call me shorty!

Fan-bloody-tastic!

Far out!

Gee whiz!

Glory be!

God almighty!

God stiffen my cat's arse!

Good God and Highlanders!

Good grief!

Good lord!

Goodness gracious!

Goodnight nurse!

Great galloping goannas!

Grouse!

Hell's bells and buckets of blood!

Holy cow! / hell! / Moses! / shit!

How about that!

Humdinger!

I'll be a monkey's uncle!

I'll be blowed! / buggered! / damned! / hanged! / stuffed!

Exclamations: Amazement and Disbelief

Jeepers, creepers!

Jesus Christ! Jeez!

Mrs Tuckfield's Tiny Tits!

My oath! My word!

Now I've seen it all!

Ripper!

Shit a brick!

Shit a brick and fart a bubble! / crowbar!

Shiver me shirt! / timbers!

Starve the crows! / lizards!

Stone the crows!

Strike a light!

Strike me lucky!

Strike me pink!

Strike me up a gum tree!

Struth!

Sugar!

Well, I'll go to the foot of the stairs!

Well, I never!

Whacko-the-diddle-oh-pig's-bum!

Wonders never cease!

Yo!

You could have knocked me down with a feather!

You don't say!

You wouldn't read about it!

Disbelief ...

All my eye and Betty Martin!
(said to be a sailor's garbled version of words heard in an Italian church, "Ah mihi, beate Martini!" – "Ah, grant me, blessed St Martin!" Now it merely means 'nonsense'.

a likely story!

Balls! Baloney!

Bull! Bullshit! Bullswool!

Break it down!

Come off it! Come off the grass!

Crap! Cocky crap!

Didn't come down in the last shower!

Exclamations: Amazement and Disbelief

Don't come that with me!
Don't come the raw prawn!
Don't make me laugh!
Garn!
Get away!
Get off the grass!
Go on!
Like buggery! Like fun!
My foot!
Phooey!
Pigs! Pig's arse! Pig's bum!
Pigs might fly!
Pull the other leg! (It's got bells on!)
Sure!

Tell that to the marines! When the British installed marines on their naval ships, the sailors were contemptuous of them – hence they could **'tell that to the marines'** because they would be gullible enough to believe anything. The term, **'dead marines'** (empty liquor bottles) was also intended as an insult - like 'dead' liquor bottles, the marines were useless (according to the sailors), and served no other purpose than to take up space on a ship.

That'll be the day!
That's a good one!
Wasn't born yesterday!
Whaddya think *this* is – Bush Week?
Yeah! Yeah!
You're putting me on!

Exclamations: Amazement and Disbelief

Fisherman: "I caught a cod in the Murray. Without a word of a lie, it was so big that by the time I got its tail out of the water, its head had gone rotten!"

"Yeah! Yeah!"

Ted was on his way home from work when his car broke down on a back road. As he began to walk towards a farmhouse in the distance, a snazzy yellow sports car pulled up beside him.

"Can I help?" asked a gorgeous blonde.

Ted explained the situation, and the young lady told him that she lived in a small town about ten miles away. She said that she would take him home for dinner, and he could phone a garage from her house. Ted readily accepted her offer – and thus it was that he eventually got his car repaired and arrived back home in the early hours of the morning.

"Where do you think *you've* been?" screamed his wife. "Out all hours, no phone call!"

"The car broke down and I was helped out by a gorgeous, young blonde in a sports car, and I ended up having dinner with her at her house, and then....."

"A likely story!" shouted his wife. "I've had enough of your lies. You've been out playing cards with the boys again!"

Faunal Lingo

bald as a bandicoot

barra (barramundi – our national fish dish name thought to be from Queensland Aboriginal language)

bit of a brumby lot (wild buggers!) A **brumby** is a wild horse – named after a Major Brumby who bred horses in the early days of white settlement. When he was transferred to Tasmania, some of his horses could not be caught and became wild. After that, wild horses became known as **'brumbies.'**

bunyip aristocracy Australia's landed gentry. A **bunyip** is a mythical creature – thus it is a slur on the new upper-class

as dry as a dead dingo's donger

as dry as a kookaburra's Khyber in the Simpson desert

done up like a pet lizard

fit as a mallee bull

flat out like a lizard drinking

game as a piss-ant

hair like a bush pig's arse

happy as a boxing kangaroo in a fog (miserable)

haven't seen him in donkey's years (long time - distortion of 'as long as donkey's ears')

kangaroos in the top paddock (crazy)

like a possum up a gum tree (very happy)

like a shag on a rock (lonely)

like a stunned mullet (bewildered)

lively as a blowie on a winter's day (lethargic)

mad as a pack of galahs

magpie (talkative / a hoarder)

mozzies (mosquitoes – so large you could hear them changing gears as they neared the house – I kid you not!)

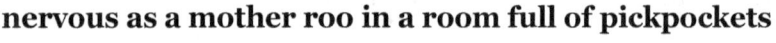

muddie: (Queensland mud-crab – proper good tucker!)

nervous as a mother roo in a room full of pickpockets

on the Murray cod (r.s. for 'on the nod', meaning 'on credit')

pissed as a parrot

play the goanna (piano)

play possum (pretend to be asleep)

a proper galah (stupid)

racecourse emu (one who scours a racecourse looking for discarded tickets)

randy as a mallee bull (very lustful)

since Cocky was an egg (long time ago)

stands out like a black crow in a bucket of milk (very obvious)

stir the possum (create a disturbance)

turn dingo (informer)

where the crows fly backwards to keep the dust out of their eyes

Bit o' Bush Wisdom

Even the head cocky
Makes a galah of himself sometimes.

The old bloke headed off to the river with his fishing rod and a bottle of whisky. As he settled down on the bank, he realized he'd forgotten the bait. Suddenly something stirred in the grass beside him. There he saw a snake with a frog in its mouth. He grabbed the snake around the neck and took the frog for bait. Because he felt a bit mean about doing this, he poured a drop of whisky down the snake's throat and hurled it into the bush. Later, as he was sitting there with his line in the river, he felt a tap on his back. He turned, and there was the snake with another frog in its mouth!

Food: Grub Or Tucker

or **chow, din-dins, feed, monger, nosh-up, spread**

If you LIKE TO EAT, you're ...

good on the fang

have hollow legs

like to pork out

So Hungry ...

I could chew the arse out of a rag doll / rhinoceros

I could chew the crutch out of an Afghan camel-driver's jocks

I could eat a baby's bum through a cane chair

I could eat the bum out of a low-flying duck

I could eat the crutch out of a nightie

I could eat a galah and bark sandwich

I could eat a goanna between two slabs of bark

I could eat a horse and chase the rider

I could eat a horse between two bread vans

I could eat a scabby horse between two lousy mattresses

I could eat a shit sandwich, but I don't like bread

I'm famished / me stomach thinks its throat's cut / that didn't touch the sides

Food: Grub Or Tucker

So Thirsty ...
('cos a man's not a camel, you know!)

I'm as dry as a camel driver's bum

I'm as dry as a cat's crack

I'm as dry as a navvy's armpit (a **navvy** is a labourer, and so he's obviously not workin' up a sweat!)

I'm as dry as a nun's whatsit

I'm as dry as a witch's tit

I'm as dry as a wood chip

If you've HAD ENOUGH TO EAT you're ...

Better Belly Bust than Good Food Wasted

chockas

had elegant sufficiency for my delicate constitution

full as a boot / bull / bull's bum

full as a butcher's dog

full as a fairy's phone book

full as a goog

full as a state-school hat rack

full as a tick

full as the family po on a Friday night

full enough to crack a flea on my stomach

full up to dolly's wax (dolls once had wax heads only)

full up to pussy's bow

F.U.R.T.B. (Full Up Ready To Bust)

me back teeth's in water

If you're **UNABLE to EAT** all that you've put on your plate:
your eyes are bigger than your belly

Food: Grub Or Tucker

What's For Dinner?

bee's knees and sparrow's ankles
bread and duck under the table
bread and scrape / bread and spit
bread and pullet
cat's poop and pepper wrapped in brown paper
duck under the table and pullet – with effort
fish hooks and rubber necks
four-course meal – bread, dripping, pepper and salt
glass of water and a canary seed
hot sun rolls and wind pudding
ifits – if it's put on the table, you'll get some
pickled eel's feet
pig's arse and cabbage / pig's bum and gooligum
pig's tit and honey
shit on bread with hundreds and thousands
shit on sugar
snake's bum on a biscuit
stewed bugs 'n onions
stewed roodleums
things you wave in the air
wait-and-see pudding
wallabadootchananapoostix
what Paddy shot at
windmill pudding – you'll get a bit if it goes around
windy cakes and ta-ta- sauce

Food: Grub Or Tucker

AUSSIE GRACE:
Two, four, six, eight,
Bog in, don't wait.
Knives and forks
As sharp as razors,
Fill your bellies,
And go like blazes!

If it Doesn't Fatten, it'll Fill

to quiet the worms, you can **tuck into:**

bangers / dodgers / mystery bags / snags / widows' memories: sausages (**'bangers'** are so-named from the

noise they make while cooking)

bill poster's paste (custard)

brekkie: (breakfast) **brunch:** (breakfast and early lunch together)

bubble and squeak: (left-over meat and vegetables)

bumnuts / cackleberries / googs / hen fruit (eggs)

bunghole (cheese)

Burdekin duck (corned beef dipped in batter and fried)

bushman's chutney (jam and Worcestershire sauce)

bush tucker (edible bush food)

caulie (cauliflower)

chew-and-spew / snatch-and-grab / take-away (take-away food)

chewie (chewing gum)

chockies (chocolate)

chook (poultry)

cocky's joy (golden syrup)

colonial goose (mutton dipped in batter and fried)

crochet-work steak (honeycomb tripe)

cuey (cucumber)

cuppa (cup of tea, coffee, etc.) If you're out in the bush, it's very 'Aussie' to **'boil a billy'** over an open fire for your cuppa. Then, to demonstrate your prowess in bushcraft, you swing the billy containing the brew around and around without (hopefully!) spilling the contents. For the less adventurous, **'to swing the billy'** now means only **'to get a cuppa'** for someone. A **'billy'** is a tin can with a wire handle. The word **'billy'** comes from the Scottish dialect, 'bally' – bally-cog', meaning 'a milk pail.'

dagwood (very large sandwich – from the comic-strip character, Dagwood, who loved to make such large sandwiches)

Dalmatian pudding (bread-'n-butter pudding with raisins)

damper (bushman's bread) Invented by William Bond, Australia's first baker. It was simply unleavened bread, made from flour and water, and baked in ashes. It got its name from the practice of **'damping a fire'**, or covering it with ashes to keep the embers burning slowly. The wet blanket of dough had much the same effect as the ashes.

dead horse (r.s.) sauce

dodger (bread - a hunka dodger is a piece of bread)

to **'know which side your bread's buttered on'** is to know where the advantage is

dog's eye(r.s.) / rat's coffin / sinker (meat pie)

pie floater (pie in pea soup or gravy – S.A. delicacy)

Food: Grub Or Tucker

dog's eye and don't-be-nasty (pie and pasty)

fart fodder (any food that causes flatulence)

flake (shark fillet)

fly bog (jam)

fly cemetery: (fruit cake)

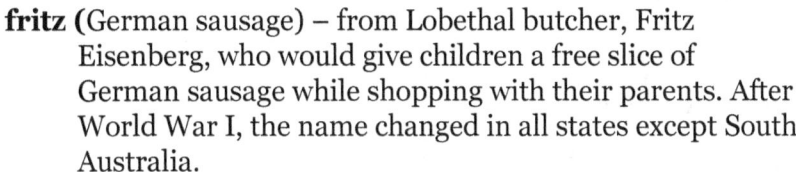

frog's eyes / spawn (sago or tapioca)

fritz (German sausage) – from Lobethal butcher, Fritz Eisenberg, who would give children a free slice of German sausage while shopping with their parents. After World War I, the name changed in all states except South Australia.

grannie (Granny Smith apple variety)

grease (butter)

husband-beater (long bread stick)

johnny-cake (type of small damper)

junk food (take-away food)

Kidman's blood mixture (treacle)

lamingtons / lammies (chocolate and coconut-covered cake – after Baron Lamington, Governor of Queensland, 1895–1901)

lollies (sweets)

lolly-water (soft-drink, lemonade)

loop-the-loop (soup)

marge (margarine)

mash (mashed potato)

moo-juice (milk)

murphies / spuds / taters (potatoes)

narna (banana)

93

parson's nose (tail-end of a fowl when cooked)

pav (pavlova – soft-centred meringue dessert) - named after Anna Pavlova, famous ballerina

prairie oysters (calf's testicles)

puftaloons (fried scones)

sambo / Sammie / sanger / sarnies (sandwich)

sand (sugar)

sav (saveloy)

snot-block (vanilla slice)

spag bog (spaghetti bolognaise)

squashed ants / worms (Vegemite – or yeast extract spread pressed through dry biscuits)

tea (main evening meal)

tinned dog (any tinned meat)

tommies (tomatoes)

underground mutton (rabbit)

Vegemite (brand name of Aussies' favourite spread made from yeast extract – developed by Cyril Callister in 1922.)

vegies (vegetables)

BREKKIE seems to be the main meal of the day in Oz, and you can select the **me'nyu** from the following:

a dingo's breakfast (bugger all)

a dog's breakfast (a pee and a trot around the yard)

a duck's breakfast (a drink and a squirt under the table)

an emu's breakfast (a drink and a good look around – one up on the dingoes!)

a jockey's breakfast (a drink and a good shit – had to lose weight!)

a mad woman's breakfast (a mess)

a pilot's breakfast (a fag and a cup of black coffee) By the way, the word **'fag'**(slang for 'cigarette') came from the textile industry. The **'fag'** was the end piece of the cloth. Small boys would call out to smokers, "Give us a **fag**, mister!" (end of their cigarettes.) **'Fag'** was also the term for the untwisted end of a piece of rope – hence the expression, **'fagged out.'**

a swaggie's breakfast (a piss and a good look around, a drink of water, a crap and tighten your belt, or a look over the shoulder and keep going)

If your dinner is **done to a turn'**, everything is complete and perfect. However, if *you're* **done like a dinner**, you're completely and utterly stuffed!

Thought you might be interested to know that we've only been stuffin' ourselves with three meals a day since the Victorian Age. We always had brekkie 'to break one's fast,' and dinner has gradually moved from midday to after sundown (probably accounts for we oldies speaking of 'dinner' for what is now known as 'lunch'), but it wasn't until after the division of the Victorian working day into two periods (from 9 a.m. to 1 p.m. and from 2 p.m. to 6 p.m.) that luncheon became an institution.

Two missionaries in Africa were captured by a tribe of hostile cannibals who put them in a large pot of water, built a fire under it, and left them there. As the water boiled and the heat grew more intense, one of the missionaries began to laugh hysterically. The other missionary couldn't believe it!

He said, "What's wrong with you? We're being cooked alive! They're going to eat us! What could possibly be funny at a time like this?"

The other missionary smiled. "I just pissed in the soup!"

Food: Grub Or Tucker

Bit o' Bush Wisdom

**If you carry on like a pork chop,
Chances are that you'll end up covered in gravy.**

A townie arrived at an outback town after a long drive in the heat and dust. He settled down on a chair in the only café in town, and it was then that he noticed that the menu was rather strange. All that was on it was ham sandwiches, roast pork, pig's trotters, eggs and bacon, and pork chops. Suddenly his appetite deserted him.

"I'll just have a glass of water, thanks," he told the waitress.

"I think I ought to warn you that we only have bore water," said the waitress.

"Stone the flamin' crows!" he shouted, "You sure don't waste much of that pig!"

Galahs, Galoots And Other Idiots

We just love to insult each other. In Oz it's often a sign of great affection as well as dislike. While living overseas, our son would ring home just to have his parents lob a few insults at him!

There's no shortage of words to choose from:

basket case

berk

bimbo (usually reserved for females)

bird-brain

blithering idiot

blockhead

bloody galah / galoot / nong

bonzo / chucklehead / chump

clod

clot

clown

crackpot

cretin

dag

dead-head

dick-head or Richard

Cranium

dill

dimwit

dingaling

dingbat

dipstick

do-dally

donkey / dope / dopey / dopey Dora

drip

drongo

duffer

dumb-bum / dumb-cluck

dumbo

dum-dum / dummy

dunce

fathead

fruitcake

Galahs, Galoots And Other Idiots

fruit-loop
geek
git
goat
goose
great ape
half-wit
jackass
jerk
klutz
knucklehead
lame-brain
loony
meatball / meathead
melon
moo
moron
mutton-head
nerd
nincompoop
ning-nong
ninny
nit-wit
nut / nutcase / nutter
pea-brain

proper galah
pudding
queer
sap
schmuck
screwball
silly sausage
silly-billy
spas
turkey
twerp
twit
wally
woodenhead
yob / yobbo

Space To Sell Between The Ears ...

a few palings off the fence

as free from brains as a frog is from feathers

actin' the goat (in ancient Greek tragedies, males were disguised as Satyrs and dressed in goat skins. However, 'actin' the goat' is not exactly a 'tragic act' now!

actin' like a pork chop

a banger short of a barbie

barmy as a bandicoot

bats in the belfry

bent as a scrub tick

brick short of a load

bright as a two-watt bulb

cotton wool between the ears

couldn't organize a fart in a baked beans factory

couldn't win if he started the night before

couple of pies short of a grand final

couple of stubbies short of a six-pack

couple of tadpoles short of a swamp

dead from the neck up

doesn't know if he's Arthur or Martha

driving uphill with the clutch slipping

few roos loose in the top paddock

going through life with the porch light on dim

got rocks in his head

hasn't enough brains to give himself a headache

hasn't enough sense to come in out of the rain

hasn't the foggiest idea

hasn't the sense he was born with

If his brains were dynamite, he wouldn't have enough powder to blow his hat off.

If his brains were elastic, they wouldn't make a set of garters for a one-legged canary.

knocking, but nobody answers

lift doesn't go to the top floor

lights are on, but there's nobody home

lost his marbles

mad as a cut snake

mad as a hatter

muscle-bound between the ears

needs his head read

non compos

not all his dogs are barking

not all there

not the full bottle / full quid

not the sharpest knife in the drawer

nothing up top

off the planet

out for lunch

out of his tree

round the bend / round the twist

a sandwich short of a picnic

silly as all get-out

silly as a tin of fish goin' fishin'

silly as a two-bob watch

silly as a wet hen / a wheel

sharp as a bowling ball

short of numbers in the Upper House

soft in the head

so slow he couldn't get a job as a speed hump

spanner short in the tool box

stubbie short of a six-pack

thick as a boarding-house sandwich

thick as a brick

thick as the dust on a public servant's out-tray

thick as two short planks

upper storey's vacant

water on the brain

white ants in the billy

wouldn't know if a band was up him till he got the drum

wouldn't know if a bus was up him till the people got off

wouldn't know his arse from a hole in the ground

Dad and Dave had made a bit of money with booming wool prices, and so they decided to spend a bit of the proceeds in the Big Smoke. They booked into a hotel and went down to the bar for a couple of pints. However, after a few more pints than intended they retired to their room, and hopped into the double bed. Soon they were both snoring loudly.

Suddenly Dad woke up, shook Dave and shouted, "Dave, I'm

as thirsty as buggery. Nip down to the bathroom and bring me back a glass of water." Dave did as he was asked, and came back with a brimming glass. Dad gulped it in one swallow and went back to sleep. After half an hour he woke again and made the same request.

The procedure was repeated throughout the night, but on the last occasion Dave returned without the water.

"Where's me drink, son?"

"Gee Dad, I'm sorry," said Dave, "but when I went down to the bathroom I couldn't get any 'cos some silly bastard was sittin' on the well!"

Mean, Miserly And Tight-Fisted

You know the type –

a penny-pincher a tight-arse mean as bird-shit / cat-shit

Mean! ...

if he owned the sea he wouldn't give you a wave

he'd skin a louse for its hide

he has a death adder in his pocket

he has short arms and deep pockets

he wouldn't give a dog a drink at his mirage

he wouldn't give a rat a railway pie

he wouldn't give him a fart to cool his soup

he wouldn't give you a fright even if he were a ghost

he wouldn't shout in a shark attack

he wouldn't show you a short cut to the shit-house even if you had the trots

he wouldn't tell you the time if he had two watches

when a fly lands in the sugar, he shakes it before he kills it

As Tight ...

as a bull's arse in fly time

as a cat's bum

as a fish's arse going upstream / in a frozen pond

as a monkey's arse

So tight ...

you couldn't drive a caraway seed up his arse with a mallet

Tighter than two coats of paint

A man buys a packet of salted peanuts and gives one to his wife. Five minutes later she asks for another one.

"Why do you want another one?" he asks. "They all taste the same."

Nicknames

Y'all know Blue, doncha – the one with the red hair?

The word **'nickname'** comes from a corrupted form of 'ekename' – 'eke' means 'additional', and so it is an additional name. Alec Gurney's famous comic strip, 'Bluey and Curley' is based on two Aussie diggers with nicknames. Aussies love to bestow nicknames, both as **a symbol of affection or as a vehicle for ridicule.** Sometimes the names are perverse, e.g. a tall man is called 'Shorty.' The surname itself may suggest the nickname, e.g. 'Coffey' becomes 'Bean' and 'Bell' becomes 'Tinker'.

Check out the following: -

Aches-and-Pains: he tells you about them in detail!

Ajax: because, like the powder, she takes everything off first time

All-Night Chemist: never shuts up

Apples: gives everyone the pip

Arnotts: he has a ginger nut

Artesian: he's a bore

Aspro: surname is Nicholas (produced 'Aspro' pain relief tablets)

Batteries: let her loose in a shop and she'll charge everything!

Battleship: sinks schooners at night

Bex: he's a real headache

Bindi-Eye: like the burr, he's hard to shake off

Blowfly: comes in the moment you leave the door open

Bot: always borrowing – unwelcome as a bot fly

Bugle: blows his own trumpet

Nicknames

Cashmere Bouquet: doesn't wash
Cattle Truck: full of bull
Chrome Dome / Nude Nut: bald
Cigarette Paper: always giving himself big wraps
Cloudy: dull and overcast
Cork: always popping in and out of the pub
Corpse: lies a lot
Crusoe: his name is Robinson
Dandruff: always getting the brush-off
Decibel: a very loud voice
Dunlop: has a huge spare tyre around his middle
Encyclopaedia: has all the answers – just ask him!
Escalator: girls say he never knows when to stop
Fertilizer: so thin he's all blood 'n bone
Foghorn: talks in whispers
Friday Legs: thin legs – (Catholics knew – no meat on Friday!)
Fruit Salts: can't tell him anything – 'E knows!
Gelding: cricketer – because of number of 'no balls' he bowls
Guillotine: he's a pain in the neck
Harpic: he's clean round the bend
H2O: a teetotaller
Hoover: he picks up any bit of fluff

Hydraulic: lift anything – even pinch the bridle off a nightmare!

Igloo: she's as cold as ice

Jolly: surname is Rogers

Kolynos: has bad breath (Kolynos was a brand of toothpaste)

Kooka: laughs at his own jokes

Laughing Armpit: a jovial bloke with large, black beard

Leader of the Opposition: the wife

Lightning: 'cos he's slow

Local Rag: town gossip

London Fog: never lifts

Lucky Legs: lucky they don't break off and stick up her arse

Ma Kettle: she's always on the boil

Martyr: he's always getting stoned

Milk Bottle: wife finds him full on the doorstep each morning

Miss World: has a figure like a globe

Nero: loves fiddling with the flaming barbecue

Neuralgia: a pain in the neck

One-Bob and Two-Bob: two chaps named Bob

Phenobarb: slow-working dope

Pickles: such a dill **Beecham's Pill (r.s.)** dill

The Pill: hard to take

Playtex: no visible means of support

Pull Through: long and skinny – as if pulled through a pipe

Rainbow: only appears when everything's finished

Rear Window: a 'pane' in the behind

Rust: she'll get into *any* car

Shadow: a pest that, like your shadow, you can't lose

The Sheep: addresses his mates as 'youse'

Short Arms: can't reach the bottom of his pockets for his shout

The Shoe: always putting his foot in it

Superstar: thinks he's Jesus Christ, himself

Three-Oh-Three: foreman known for giving workers the bullet

Titus: tight as a fish's arse

Twenty Watts: rather dim

Upper Cut: thinks he's a knock-out with the girls

Whisper: never been known to shout

Wombat: sort of bloke who eats, roots, shoots and leaves

Your Highness: always on the throne when there's work around

An over-zealous young copper took up duty in a country town. Pretty soon he was driving the locals mad, picking them up for every little law infringement. He had his eye on Cork Cameron, who occasionally used to stagger home from the local rubbidy.

One night Cork got 'caught short' in a lane on his way home from the pub. He unzipped his fly, and away he went. To his horror, he saw the copper approaching. Quick as a flash, he did up his zipper and stood there, trying to look innocent.

"Cork," said the copper sternly, "did you pass urine in this lane?"

"To tell y' th' truth, offisher," replied Cork, "I haven't sheen a shoul."

Occupations

"Whaddya do fer a crust?"

"I'm on a pretty good screw (wage) in this job."

amen snorter / Bible basher / God botherer / man of God /

sky pilot: CLERGYMAN

babbling brook (r.s.): cook **slushy:** KITCHEN-HAND

beak: MAGISTRATE / POLICEMAN

bean counter / number cruncher: ACCOUNTANT

bookie: HORSE-RACING BOOKMAKER

bottle-oh: BOTTLE COLLECTOR – adding '**o**' to a call added strength to the voice of street sellers, and so began the habit of adding '**o**' to some of our words, e.g. **milk-o, rabbit-o.** It then became the name for the vendor himself.

bouncer: employed to EVICT TROUBLE-MAKERS

brickie: BRICKLAYER

brown bomber(N.S.W.) / grey ghost: PARKING INSPECTOR

bush carpenter: UNQUALIFIED CARPENTER

cabbie: TAXI-DRIVER

chalkie / schoolie: SCHOOL TEACHER a **chalkie** was also a CLERK who used to chalk up prices at the Stock Exchange.

check-out chick: CASH-REGISTER OPERATOR at a store

chippie: CARPENTER

Occupations

chiro: CHIROPRACTOR

cockatoo: GUARD outside illegal gambling joint - now obsolete

cocky: FARMER – from idea that a farmer tried to scratch a living from a patch of bare earth

cop / flatfoot / fuzz / john / pig / walloper: POLICEMAN

cow-cocky: DAIRY FARMER

dick: DETECTIVE

DJ : DISC-JOCKEY

dogger: DINGO HUNTER

duffer: CATTLE THIEF
    poddy dodger: thief who specializes in calves

ducks and geese (r.s.) POLICE

dunny diver / turd strangler: PLUMBER

fang farrier: DENTIST

fence: DEALER in STOLEN GOODS

garbo: GARBAGE COLLECTOR

grease monkey: MECHANIC

greasy: OUTBACK COOK / SHEEP SHEARER

gun: TOP PICKER or SHEARER

gyno: GYNAECOLOGIST

head-shrinker / shrink: PSYCHIATRIST

honey-dipper / sanno: LAVATORY CLEANER

hooker / mallee root: PROSTITUTE

hoop: JOCKEY

hostie: AIR-HOSTESS

jackeroo / jillaroo (female) SHEEP/CATTLE STATION WORKER

'Jackeroo' is said to have come from 'Jackie Raw,' the name given to a new recruit on a station. 'Jack' was a common name ('every man jack of you') and the new chums were certainly 'raw!' By substituting 'roo' for 'raw' it made them uniquely Australian.

journo: JOURNALIST

land-shark: LAND SPECULATOR

legal-eagle: LAWYER / SOLICITOR

man in white: SPORTS UMPIRE

medico / quack: DOCTOR 'Quack' is a shortened form of 'quacksalver' – one who fraudulently sold ointments (they 'quacked' loudly about the so-called benefits of what they were selling.) Term is now used for any medicos.

milkie / milko: MILK VENDOR

muso: MUSICIAN

pen-pusher: CLERK / WRITER

pick-and-shovel man: LABOURER

pollies: POLITICIANS

postie: POSTMAN

pox-doctor: VENEREAL DISEASE SPECIALIST

pug: BOXER

rep: TRAVELLING SALESMAN

ringer: DROVER, STATION-HAND, STOCKMAN

Occupations

salt: EXPERIENCED SEAMAN **tar:** SAILOR

sawbones: SURGEON

shiny-arse: PUBLIC SERVANT

sparkie: ELECTRICIAN

speed-cop: POLICEMAN who enforces ROAD LAWS

squatter: PASTORALIST – formerly a person who settled on Crown land to run stock (usually sheep) without legal title

subbie: SUB-CONTRACTOR

trammie: TRAM CONDUCTOR

truckie: TRUCK DRIVER

vet: VETERINARIAN

wharfie: WHARF LABOURER

wrecker: DEMOLISHES CARS, HOUSES

At a level crossing a train clipped the rear of a fully-laden night-cart. A lady came by and watched the night-carter cleaning up the mess with a shovel. Handkerchief over her nose, the lady asked, "Have you had an accident?"

"Nah, lady, I'm just stocktaking."

Bit o' Bush Wisdom

**Some people are like a callous –
They always show up when the work is done.**

"Roll up! Roll up! Buy this miraculous cure for your old age. Rigor mortis can be cured! Roll up! Roll up!" called the fairground quack.

He soon collected a large crowd, all curious to hear his spiel. "You only have to look at me," he went on, "to see the proof. I am over two hundred and fifty years old."

One man in the crowd turned to the quack's beautiful young assistant and said, "Is that true? Is he *really* over two hundred and fifty years old?"

"I'm afraid I can't say," replied the quack's assistant. "I've only been working for him for the past ninety-three years."

Did you know that in the early days of the Industrial Revolution craftsmen had to supply their own tools of trade? If they were dismissed, their employer had to give them a sack in which to take their tools away – hence the expression, **'to get the sack.'**

Rabbit And Pork (Talk)

She'd **talk under wet cement with a mouthful of marbles**, her favourite dish is **tongue pie**, and she belongs to the **CWA (Chin Waggers' Association.)**

To be fair, men also like **'to have a bit of a yarn,'** and some are only too happy **'to take the floor'** and **'blow down your ear.'**

You May ...

be a gabble-guts / gabby (talkative)

be a gas-bag (incessant talker)

be a wind-bag (excessive, empty talk)

be the talk of the town (subject of rumour, gossip)

have enough jaw for another row of teeth

have the gift of the gab (glib speech)

have verbal diarrhoea (run at the mouth – non-stop talk)

prattle / waffle on (talk a lot about nothing in particular)

yabber (chatter) **yackety-yak** (idle talk)

You May Like To Have ...

a chat / a chin-wag / a mag (from 'magpie,' bird that has a reputation for 'talking' a lot), **a pow-wow**, or **a yarn**

dirty yarn (vulgar story)

shaggy-dog story (long, involved, funny story)

spin a yarn (tell a story)

tall story (far-fetched, unlikely to be true)

You May Like ...

chewin' the fat

flappin' the gums (gossiping)

tellin' it like it is (the truth – as you see it)

walkin' the talk (practicing what you preach)

You May Talk ...

a lot of crap (rubbish)

a lot of hot air (boastful talk, nonsense)

as if you have a plum in your mouth (affected speech)

as if your lip is bleeding (use big words)

as if you were vaccinated with a gramophone needle (non-stop)

back (answer impertinently)

behind someone's back (make unkind remarks in their absence)

big (boast)

double-Dutch (gibberish) In the 17th century, when the Dutch and English were at loggerheads for maritime trade, there were a number of verbal put-downs, e.g. **Dutch wife** (mattress)

down to (condescending)

like a butcher's magpie (talkative)

nineteen to the dozen (fast, difficult to understand)

off the top of your head / through your hat (nonsense)

shop (discuss business, job, profession)

someone blind / chew someone's ear (bore them to tears)

someone into something / someone round (persuade)

the leg off an iron pot (incessantly)

turkey (serious discussion)

underwater with a snorkel on (and that's talking!)

your head off (speak at great length)

Put-Downs ...

To someone who butts in or offers unwanted advice:

I want to talk to the butcher, not the block.

I want to talk to the engineer, not the oily rag.

If you RING SOMEONE on the **Al Capone / dog-and-bone / eau-de-cologne (r.s.)** TELEPHONE, you may **'give them a bell'** or **'a tingle.'**

Tell ...

me about it! (emphatic agreement)

(someone) a thing or two, (someone) off (reprimand)

on someone (inform)

tell tales out of school (betray confidences)

Tell you what! (often precedes an assertion)

Ruminating Riddle

**Why do men pass more gas than women?
Because women won't shut up long enough to build up pressure.**

Bit o' Bush Wisdom

**If you chew on a problem long enough,
You'll end up spitting chips.**

I haven't spoken to my wife for 18 months; I don't like to interrupt her.

A bloke was giving a speech at a Rotary club, and he got a bit carried away and waffled on for three hours. Realising that he had been a bit long-winded, he apologized, "I'm terribly sorry I talked so long. I forgot to wear my watch."

A bloke at the back of the room piped up, "Well, you could have at least looked at the bloody calendar behind you once or twice!"

Thingamabobs And Whatsanames

We Aussies seem to have a bit lacking in the memory department, as we have a number of words for things that we have temporarily forgotten.

Bet you can identify with the following:-

antiwontigon

doodad

doohickey

doojigger

doover / dooverbug

dooverlackey

goankipike

jigamatite

junk / stuff

oojahkapivvy

padidgiewacker

so-and-so

thingy

thing you hang the moon up with

watchamacallit

whatjamaflop

whatshisface

whatsit

whomajigger

whatnot

wigwam for a goose's bridle (also a common put-down to children in answer to the question, **"What is it?"**)

"Where is it?" "Up in Annie's room, behind the clock."

"Where are you going, Mum?"

"Out of my mind – want to come with me?"

Dave and Mabel were out walking along the river bank one afternoon when they came across Herb Wilson sitting by a large gum tree with a fishing line in the river.

"Are yer catchin' any?" asked Dave.

"A few," said Herb.

"Ow big?" asked Dave.

"Only tiddlers," said Herb, "about the size of your little watchamacallit."

Dave and Mabel retreated to the other side of the tree and started to have a smooch.

Shortly after Mabel called out to Herb. "Eh, Herb!" she giggled.

"Yes, Mabel."

"Betcha catchin' some whoppers, now!"

Useful or Useless as –

Aussies are not highly regarded as 'culture-vultures', but there is something picturesque about the following colloquialisms.

as USEFUL as ...

a blackberry patch in a nudist camp

a chocolate teapot

a dog, chook, or man with tits

a glass door on a dunny

a wooden oven

tits on Tarzan

as USELESS as ...

a fly-wire door on a submarine

an ash-tray on a motor-bike

a one-legged man in an arse-kicking contest

a pocket in a singlet

a prostitute at a poofter's wedding

a spare prick at a wedding

a windscreen-wiper on a submarine

the bottom half of a mermaid

Useful or Useless as –

No Use nor Ornament

not much chop

not worth a brass razoo / damn

not worth a bumper

not worth a fart in a noisemaker / thunderstorm

not worth a pinch of goat-shit / shit

not worth a rat's arse

not worth feeding

not worth one's salt The Romans paid part of their soldiers' wages in salt. This was later changed to a cash allowance so that they could buy their own salt – a very important commodity. The word 'salarium' or 'salt allowance' came to mean 'payment for services' or 'salary.'

'not worth one's salt - 'not worth one's pay'

not worth the paper it's written on

not worth thinking about

An international committee of women has announced that computers should be referred to as masculine because:

(a) In order to get their attention you have to turn them on.
(b) They have a lot of data but are still clueless.
(c) Instead of helping you solve problems, they ***are*** the problem.
(d) As soon as you make a commitment to one, you realize that if you'd waited a little longer, you could have had a better model.

Weather: "Send 'Er Down, Hughie!"

Maybe it's because we live on the driest continent on earth that we're so interested in the weather. The impassioned appeal for rain, **"Send 'er down, Hughie!"** has been in use for yonks. The origin of 'Hughie' is uncertain, although there are several explanations.

(1) from the aboriginal, "Send it down, Yowie!" ('Yowie' is the word for 'thunder.')

(2) a former government meteorologist was Hughie Watt.

(3) an ardent early water conservationist was Hughie McColl, who came from Bendigo, in Victoria.

(4) Hugh Trumble, a fast bowler whose fans would cry, **"Send 'er down, Hughie – wooden legs are cheap!"**

(Cricket is the **other Aussie religion.** The game was first played in England (where else?) by shepherds as a pastime while minding sheep. They bowled at two uprights and a cross-bar that rested on the slotted tops. The cross-bar was called a 'bail', and the gate a 'wicket.' The first recorded match was in 1697, and of course, the Poms who arrived in the First Fleet in 1788 didn't take long to bowl their first 'maiden over' (sorry!).

Whatever, the origin of the name, it has become a jocular, if irreverent reference to the deity – **"Blame it on Hughie!" "Hughie did it!"**

If it's COLD it's ...

as cold and dark as a bushman's grave

as cold as a frog's tit

as cold as a polar bear's bum

as cold as a well-digger's arse

cold enough to freeze the balls off a billiard table

cold enough to freeze the balls off a brass monkey

cold enough to freeze the hind legs off a donkey

cold enough to freeze the walls off a bark humpy (corruption of 'balls off a brass monkey')

If it's DUSTY it's ...

a **Wilcannia shower** (dust storm)

bite the dust (fall heavily)

couldn't see him for dust (speedy departure)

dust-off (bring out of storage)

dust-up (a fight)

If it's DRY it's ...

as dry as a dead dingo's donger dangling in the dust

as dry as a kookaburra in the Simpson Desert

as dry as a Pommy's bath towel

as dry as a stone god

as dry as a sun-struck bone

as parched as an Arab's armpit

so dry that even the kid's rocking horse is dying

so dry that there's a family of frogs under the house, and none of 'em can swim

so dry the trees are chasing the dogs

so dry there's not enough rain to christen a frog

so dry they have to staple the stamps on the letters

If it's HOT it's ...

as hot as blazes / buggery / hell

a roaster / scorcher / sizzler / swelterer

peas-in-the-pot (r.s.) (hot)

so hot I'm not fat, I'm dripping!

so hot the birds lay eggs hard-boiled

so hot the flamin' fish are perspirin' and causin' the Murray to rise

so hot the fleas and flies have bloodshot eyes from squinting

so hot the crows and hawks have sunburnt toes

If it's WET it's ...

a gundabluey (big rain storm)

Andy Cain / pleasure and pain (r.s.) (rain)

bucketing down / pissing down

drizzling (light rain)

raining cats and dogs There are several theories of the origin of this expression. In 17 century England when numerous cats and dogs ran wild, many of them were found drowned after cloudbursts, their corpses floating in the filthy torrents that rushed down the streets. It was thought that they had actually come down with the rain – hence, **'rained cats and dogs.'**

In ancient times it was believed that cats were responsible for storms, and that witches rode the storms with their black cats. Dogs were regarded as symbols of the wind and are often pictured with the Norse god, Odin. Thus cats and dogs symbolized the wind and the storm.

spitting (raining lightly)

The Wet (rainy season in tropical climates)

wet enough to bog a duck

as slow as a wet week

If it was raining film stars, you'd end up with Lassie.

If it was raining palaces, you'd get hit on the head by the dunny door.

If it was raining pea soup, you'd only have a fork.

If it was raining virgins, you'd be locked in the dunny with a poofter - all of which makes you DEAD UNLUCKY!

If it's WINDY it's ...

an Irish hurricane (dead calm)

blowing great guns

enough to blow the dog off heat

enough to blow the dog off his chain, and the fleas off the dog

> Whatever the weather, it's advisable
> to **'keep a weather eye open'** (be alert), so that you can
> **'weather any storm'** (endure, survive any difficulties)

Bit o' Bush Wisdom

Let your temper be like a bush track;
The dust flies high, but settles quickly.

An American landed one night in a little town back o'Bourke,

He called at the town's only café and had a meal. As he was leaving, he asked the owner, "Do you think it will rain?"

"Hope so," said the owner, peering up at the sky. "Not so much for my sake as the boy's. I've seen it rain."

Weather Woes ...

Just to give you some idea of how bad the drought was – the grass was so scarce the rabbits had to eat on the run to keep from starving to death.

The calves were so thin we had to tie knots in their tails to stop 'em crawlin' through the wire-netting fence.

So wet that when our Black Orpington rooster started chasin' a hen, they hadn't taken three steps before they was bogged to the bloody armpits!

The wind blew so hard the creek ran backwards for three days. It put the mill wheel in reverse and, before we could disengage it, it unground 500 bags of flour back into wheat.

It was so cold that when I shot at a hawk that was after my chickens, the bullet froze in mid-air.

Things were so tough during the last drought that the council had to close two lanes of the swimming pool.

Zacks, Deeners And Fiddley-Dids

Before decimal currency was adopted in 1966 we had very individual names for our coinage, largely derived from corruptions of French and German adopted by our soldiers during the First World War. Since 1966 we haven't come up with a single word to distinguish our currency (the word 'buck,' meaning 'a dollar' is an Americanism from their days of trading in buckskin, and is thus not relevant to Australia.) The word 'dollar' came from Germany, where a silver coin was called a 'Joachimsdaler,' or commonly known as a 'daler.'

For all those who can remember: -

1/2d. – **oddie**

1d. – **bronze** / **cobar** (from Cobar, a N.S.W. mining town - a **'sunburnt two-bob'**)

3d. – **tray (Alma Gray, Bobby Gray (r.s.), joey** (as it was small), **pen** / **scrum** / **trezzie**

6d. – **zack, (and r.s. – Andy Mac** / **Jill and Jack, hammer and tack** / **I'll be back)**

1s. – **deener, (**and **r.s. – Riverina** / **Murrumbeena), rogan** – from English combination of **'rogue'** and **'villain'** / **bob** / **colonial Robert** (play on **'bob'), joe** or **John Dillon (r.s. 'shillin')**

2s. – **sway, swy (**from **German 'zwei',** meaning **'two'.** The game of **'swy'** or **'two-up'** came from this)

10s. – **half a flag** / **half a neddie** / **half a toad** / **half a yid (r.s. – 'quid'), reddie** / **sane** (from German, **'zehn'**, ten), **ten bob** / **ten holes**

1 pound – **carpet** / **cracker** / **fiddley, fiddley-did (r.s. 'quid') flag** / **frog** / **jim (** English, **jimmy o'goblin,** a 'sovereign'), **quid** / **tiddley (r.s. 'fiddley'), smacker** / **yid** (Jewish)

5 pounds – blueback / bluey / fiver / spin / spinner / spinnaker

10 pounds – brick / red'arry / salmon

25 pounds – lifer / pony

50 pounds – half a spot / two ponies / monkey

100 pounds – four ponies / spot

500 pounds – an ape

1,000 pounds – grand / winky

a bad penny: unwanted person or thing

a penny for your thoughts: request to someone in pensive mood

big bickies / motsa (Jewish) lots of money

brass: money

brass razoo (worthless – 'haven't got a brass razoo!')

dip south: search in one's pockets for money

dough: money **do one's dough:** lose, squander, or waste money

down to one's bottom dollar: end of one's finances

down to one's last penny

hasn't got a penny to bless himself with: destitute

hasn't got a penny to his name: broke

hum: borrow or scrounge

in for a penny, in for a pound: commit oneself entirely

lucre: money

must have cost a pretty penny: must have been expensive

not worth a cracker: worthless (a **'cracker'** was a pound or quid)

not worth a tuppeny damn: no good

not worth a zack, tuppence or two bob: useless

only eighteen bob in the pound: crazy / mad

peanuts: small, insignificant amount of money

penny dreadful: cheap or sensational literature

penny finally dropped: sudden comprehension

put the acid on / put the bite on / put the fangs in: put pressure on for a loan

spend a penny: go to the toilet (women used to be charged a penny for the use of public toilets)

My horse loves to gamble.
   Every time he comes to a fence, he tosses me for it.

Farmer's Lament

It all started back in 1966 when they changed from pounds to dollars.
My bloody overdraft doubled!
Then they brought in kilograms instead of pounds.
My bloody wool clip dropped by half!
Then they changed rain to millimetres, and we haven't had an inch of rain since!
They bring in Celsius, and it never gets over 40 degrees.
No wonder my bloody wheat won't grow!
Then they change acres to hectares,
and I end up with half the bloody land I had!
By this time I'd decided to sell out. I just get the place in the agent's hands when they changed from miles to kilometres.
Now I'm too far out of town for anyone to buy the bloody place!

www.ingramcontent.com/pod-product-compliance
Lightning Source LLC
Chambersburg PA
CBHW072051290426
44110CB00014B/1642